LIMINAL SPACES

Liminal Spaces

Migration and Women of the Guyanese Diaspora

Edited by
Grace Aneiza Ali

OpenBook
Publishers

https://www.openbookpublishers.com

ISBN Paperback: 978-1-78374-987-4

ISBN Hardback: 978-1-78374-988-1

ISBN Digital (PDF): 978-1-78374-989-8

ISBN Digital ebook (epub): 978-1-78374-990-4

ISBN Digital ebook (mobi): 978-1-78374-991-1

ISBN Digital (XML): 978-1-78374-992-8

DOI: 10.11647/OBP.0218

Cover image: Grace Aneiza Ali, *The SeaWall*, Georgetown, Guyana (2014). Digital photo by Candace Ali-Lindsay. Courtesy of the artist, CC BY-NC-ND.
Cover design: Linda Florio and Anna Gatti.

Contents

for our mothers,
and their mothers

Ingrid Ali
Christina Elizabeth Baird
Dina Sheridan Benn
Khira Binda
Carmen Noreen Brewster
Doris Evelyn Brewster
Adelaide Aleta Bullen
Angela DeFreitas
Cita DeFreitas
Mae Gajee
Joyce Norma Greenidge Griffith
Patricia Kingston Gaskin Greenidge
Gertrude Elizabeth Henry Hopkinson
Aldora Hunter
Lorraine Hunter
Agatha Mewlyn Kennedy
Alma Patricia Kennedy-Scarville
Stella Knights
Enid Lewis
Lucille Badoura Mackhrandilal
Vijaya Lorna Mackrandilal
Anarkalia Mattai
Subhadra Mattai
Rita Mohamed
Rosamund Neptune
Iris Worrell-Nichols
Sara Persaud
Inez Persaud
Sarawsati Singh
Ameena Swain
Doreen U. Wilkinson
Miriam Angelina Wilkinson
Pearlene Vesta Wilkinson

Notes on the Contributors

Grace Aneiza Ali

Grace Aneiza Ali is a Curator and an Assistant Professor and Provost Fellow in the Department of Art & Public Policy at the Tisch School of the Arts at New York University in New York City. Ali's curatorial research practice centers on socially engaged art practices, global contemporary art, and art of the Caribbean Diaspora, with a focus on her homeland Guyana. She serves as Curator-at-Large for the Caribbean Cultural Center African Diaspora Institute in New York. She is Founder and Curator of *Guyana Modern*, an online platform for contemporary arts and culture of Guyana and Founder and Editorial Director of *OF NOTE Magazine*—an award-winning nonprofit arts journalism initiative reporting on the intersection of art and activism. Her awards and fellowships include NYU Provost Faculty Fellow, Andy Warhol Foundation Curatorial Fellow, and Fulbright Scholar. She has been named a World Economic Forum 'Global Shaper.' Ali was born in Guyana and migrated to the United States with her family when she was fourteen years old.

Khadija Benn

Khadija Benn was born in Canada to Guyanese parents and currently lives and works in Guyana as a geospatial analyst. She is a faculty member of the Department of Geography at the Faculty of Earth and Environmental Sciences, University of Guyana. Her research focuses on digital cartography, community development, and place attachment. As a self-taught photographer, her practice is formed around portraiture and documentary work. Her images have been exhibited at Aljira, a Center for Contemporary Art (USA), CARIFESTA XIII (Barbados), the Caribbean Cultural Center African Diaspora Institute (USA), and Addis Foto Fest (Ethiopia); and featured in *ARC Magazine* and *Transition Magazine*.

Sandra Brewster

Sandra Brewster is a Canadian visual artist based in Toronto. Her work explores identity, representation and memory, and centering Black presence. The daughter of Guyanese-born parents, she is especially attuned to the experiences of people of Caribbean heritage and their ongoing relationships with their homelands. Brewster's work has been featured in the Art Gallery of Ontario (2019-2020), she is the 2018 recipient of the Toronto Friends of the Visual Arts Artist Prize and her exhibition *It's all a blur . . .* received the Gattuso Prize for outstanding featured exhibition at the CONTACT Photography Festival 2017. Brewster holds a Master of Visual Studies from the University of Toronto. She is represented by Georgia Scherman Projects.

Erika DeFreitas

Erika DeFreitas was born in Canada. Her mother migrated from Guyana to Canada in 1970. As a Scarborough-based artist, her practice includes the use of performance, photography, video, installation, textiles, works on paper, and writing. Placing an emphasis on process, gesture, the body, documentation, and paranormal phenomena, she works through attempts to understand concepts of loss, post-memory, inheritance, and objecthood. DeFreitas' work has been exhibited nationally and internationally. She was the recipient of the TFVA 2016 Finalist Artist Prize, the 2016 John Hartman Award, and longlisted for the 2017 Sobey Art Award. DeFreitas holds a Master of Visual Studies from the University of Toronto.

Ingrid Griffith

Ingrid Griffith, writer and actor, migrated to the United States from Guyana as an adolescent in 1974. Her experiences as a child in Guyana and an immigrant in the United States have formed the wellspring of her creative inspiration. Griffith has appeared in Off-Broadway theatrical productions in classical and contemporary roles. In 2014, she debuted her first solo show at Manhattan International Theater Festival. The award-winning and internationally successful, *Demerara Gold*, is about a Caribbean girl's immigrant experience; *Demerara Gold* was published by NoPassport Press in 2016. Griffith's recently crafted solo show, titled *Unbossed & Unbowed*, explores the life of Shirley Chisholm, the first Black Congresswoman in US history. In March 2020, *Unbossed & Unbowed* debuted at Hear Her Call Caribbean-American Women's

Theater Festival where Griffith won an award for Outstanding Playwriting. Griffith teaches Public Speaking and Theater History at John Jay College of Criminal Justice in New York City. The chapter included in this anthology will be part of her soon to be finished memoir.

Natalie Hopkinson

Natalie Hopkinson, PhD, is the Canadian-born daughter of Serena Hopkinson. She is an Assistant Professor in the doctoral program of the Communication, Culture and Media Studies department at Howard University, a fellow of the Interactivity Foundation, and a former editor, staff writer, and culture and media critic at *The Washington Post* and *The Root*. Her third book of essays, *A Mouth is Always Muzzled* (2018) is about contemporary art and politics in Guyana. She lives with her family in Washington, DC.

Serena Hopkinson

Serena Hopkinson is a retired accountant and arts administrator, and a graduate of Florida Atlantic University. She grew up on the Pomeroon River in Guyana. She is a mother of four, grandmother of six, and a fierce competitor on the tennis court.

Dominique Hunter

Dominique Hunter is a multi-disciplinary artist who lives and works in Guyana, where she was born. Her artistic practice critiques the (non)-representation of Black female bodies in art history and stereotypical portrayals in contemporary print media. Her recent work has expanded to include strategies for coping with the weight of those impositions by examining the value of self-care practices. Hunter has exhibited both in the Caribbean and in the US. She has been an Artist-in-Residence with Caribbean Linked IV and the Vermont Studio Center, where she was awarded the Reed Foundation Fellowship.

Maria del Pilar Kaladeen

Maria del Pilar Kaladeen was born and currently lives in London. She is an Associate Fellow at the Institute of Commonwealth Studies in London working on the system of indenture in Guyana and its representation in literature. Having left school at fifteen and returned to education as an adult, she went on to receive a PhD in English Literature from the University of London in 2013. She is the co-editor of *We Mark Your Memory* (2018), the first international anthology on the system of indenture in the British Empire. Her life-writing has been published in *Wasafiri* and the anthology *Mother Country: Real Stories of the Windrush Children* (2018), which was longlisted for the Jhalak Prize in 2019.

Maya Mackrandilal

Maya Mackrandilal is an American-born transdisciplinary artist and writer based in Los Angeles. Mackrandilal holds an MFA from the School of the Art Institute of Chicago, where she was a recipient of a Jacob K. Javits Fellowship, and a BA from the University of Virginia, where she was a recipient of an Auspaugh Post-Baccalaureate Fellowship. Her artwork has been shown nationally, including the Chicago Artists Coalition (where she was a HATCH Artist-in-Residence), Smack Mellon, THE MISSION, Abrons Art Center, The Los Angeles Municipal Art Gallery, and the Armory Center for the Arts. She has presented artwork and research at national conferences, including the College Art Association, Association for Asian American Studies, the Critical Mixed Race Studies Association, and Open Engagement. Her writing, which explores issues of race, gender, and labor, has appeared in a variety of publications, including *The New Inquiry, Drunken Boat, contemptorary, Skin Deep*, and *MICE Magazine*.

Suchitra Mattai

Suchitra Mattai was born in Guyana in 1973 and first migrated to Canada with her family in 1976 before they came to the US. Mattai received an MFA in painting and drawing and an MA in South Asian art, both from the University of Pennsylvania, Philadelphia. Her work has appeared in various online and print publications such as *Hyperallergic, Document Journal, Cultured Magazine, Wallpaper Magazine, Harper's Bazaar Arabia, Entropy Magazine, The Daily Serving*, and *New American Paintings*. Mattai has been exhibited nationally and internationally including at the Sharjah

Biennial 14, *State of the Art 2020* at Crystal Bridges Museum/the Momentary, Denver Art Museum/Biennial of the Americas, Museum of Contemporary Art Denver, the Center on Contemporary Art Seattle, and the Art Museum of the Americas, among others.

Christie Neptune

Christie Neptune is an interdisciplinary artist working across film, photography, mixed media and performance arts. Her family migrated from Guyana to New York. Neptune holds a BA from Fordham University, New York City. Her films and photography have been included in shows at BASS Museum, Miami (2019); the University of Massachusetts Boston (2018); Rubber Factory, New York (2017); A.I.R. Gallery, Brooklyn, New York (2016); and Rutgers University (2015) among others. She has been featured in publications including *Artforum*, *Hyperallergic*, *Juxtapoze Magazine*, and *The Washington Post*. Neptune has been awarded the More Art Engaging Artist Residency, The Hamiltonian Gallery Fellowship, The Bronx Museum of the Arts: Artist in Marketplace (AIM), Smack Mellon Studio Residency through the New York Community Trust Van Lier Fellowship, The New York Foundation for the Arts (NYFA) Fellowship, and The NXTHVN Studio Fellowship. Neptune is currently an Artists Alliance Inc. LES Studio Program Artist-in-Residence.

Grace Nichols

Grace Nichols was born and educated in Guyana. Since migrating to England in 1977, she has written award-winning poetry collections and anthologies for both adults and children. Her first collection, *I is a Long Memoried Woman* (1983) won the 1983 Commonwealth Poetry Prize. Other poetry collections include, *The Fat Black Woman's Poems* (1984), *Sunris* (1996)—which won the 1997 Guyana Poetry Prize—and *Startling the Flying Fish* (2005), are all published by Virago. Her adult novel, *Whole of a Morning Sky* (1986) is set in Guyana. Her poetry collections *Picasso, I Want My Face Back* (2009), *I Have Crossed an Ocean: Selected Poems* (2010), *The Insomnia Poems* (2017), and the most recent, *Passport to Here and There* (2020), are all published by Bloodaxe Books. Nichols was the Poet-in-Residence at the University of the West Indies, Cave Hill, Barbados and at the Tate Gallery, London, 1999-2000. She received a Cholmondeley Award for her work and an Honorary Doctorate from the University of Hull. She is a fellow of the Royal Society of Literature.

Keisha Scarville

Keisha Scarville was born to Guyanese parents who migrated to the US in the 1960s. She is a photo and mixed media artist based in Brooklyn, New York and Adjunct Faculty at the International Center of Photography. Her work has been exhibited at the Studio Museum of Harlem, Rush Arts Gallery, BRIC, Aljira, a Center for Contemporary Art, Museum of Contemporary Diasporan Arts, and The Brooklyn Museum of Art. Her work has been featured in *The New York Times*, *The Village Voice*, *Hyperallergic*, *Vice*, and *Transition*, among others. Scarville has been awarded various residencies, including from the Skowhegan School of Painting and Sculpture, Vermont Studio Center, and Baxter Street CCNY.

Michelle Joan Wilkinson

Michelle Joan Wilkinson, PhD, is a writer and curator of Guyanese descent. As a Curator at the Smithsonian Institution National Museum of African American History and Culture in Washington, DC, she works on projects related to contemporary Black life and architecture and design. In her previous roles, she curated over twenty exhibitions, including two award-winning shows: *For Whom It Stands: The Flag and the American People* and *Material Girls: Contemporary Black Women Artists*. Wilkinson holds a B.A. from Bryn Mawr College and a PhD from Emory University. In 2012, she was a fellow of the Center for Curatorial Leadership, for which she completed a short-term residency at the Design Museum in London. From 2019–2020, she was a Loeb Fellow at Harvard Graduate School of Design.

Introduction: Liminal Spaces

—

Grace Aneiza Ali

How was it that till questioned, till displaced in the attempt to answer,
I had scarcely thought of myself as having a country, or indeed as having
left a country?

Vahni Capildeo, 'Going Nowhere, Getting Somewhere'[1]

In 1995, my mother, father, older brother, younger sister, and I migrated from Guyana to the United States. We became part of what seemed like a *mythical diaspora*. It is estimated that more than one million Guyanese citizens now live in global metropolises like London, Toronto, and New York City, where they are the fifth largest immigrant group.[2] Guyana itself has a modest population of approximately 787,000.[3] Yet, for a country of its small size, it has one of the world's highest out-migration rates.[4] Having gained independence from the British in 1966, Guyana has spent the last fifty-four years trying to carve out its place on the world stage. Yet Guyanese people have long known migration as the single most defining narrative of our country. We are left to grapple with the question: When we have more Guyanese living outside the country than within its borders, what becomes of our homeland?

Since its independence from British colonial rule, the last five decades in Guyana have been defined by an extraordinary ebb and flow of its citizens.[5] In an episode of the BBC Radio series *Neither Here Nor There*, host David Dabydeen, the British-Guyanese writer who left Guyana and migrated to England in 1969, examined the tremendous growth of the Guyanese diaspora since its independence. He remarked that Guyana 'is a disappearing nation' that has 'to an unrivaled degree, exported its people.'[6] The young nation continues to grapple with the remnants of a colonial past and a postcolonial present: entrenched poverty, political corruption, repressive government regimes, racial violence, lack of education, unemployment, economic depression, and a withering away of hope for a thriving future for the country.

For those who leave one place for another, impelled by choice or trauma, remaining connected to a homeland is at once beautiful, fraught, disruptive, and evolving. Making the journey with my family when we left was a handful of photographs. For many

                    https://doi.org/10.11647/OBP.0218.20

Figure I.1

My mother Ingrid (center in floral pink dress) poses with her mother, aunts, and sister at Timehri International Airport, Guyana in the 1970s, as she bade farewell to a sister who was leaving for Barbados. Persaud Family Collection.

families like mine who were poor with few possessions, owning photographs was a privilege; they were among our most valuable things.

We had no negatives, no JPEGs, no double copies—just originals. Decades later, these photographs serve as a tangible connection to a homeland left behind. In her novel *White Teeth*, the British-born writer of Jamaican heritage Zadie Smith writes, 'The end is simply the beginning of an even longer story.'[7] Indeed, the family photograph (Fig. I.1) taken at Guyana's Timehri International Airport in the 1970s captures a moment in time between concluding an old life and preparing for a new one. In the photograph, my mother (center in floral pink dress), in her early twenties at the time, poses with her mother, aunts and elder sister. They are bidding farewell to her sister (back row) who was leaving for Barbados, and who would later embark on a second migration to Canada. For the next two decades, as she grappled with a stifling poverty gripping many Guyanese, as well as the loss of her parents, my mother watched as her brothers and sisters, one by one, boarded planes to leave Guyana for neighboring Caribbean islands, and then later for Canada and the US, using student visas, work visas, marriage visas—whatever it took. The photograph reveals movement and transition as the constants in our lives where airports often served as sites for family reunions. Before I too boarded my first plane at age fourteen to depart Guyana on a one-way flight bound for New York's JFK Airport, I had long resented planes as the violent machines that fragmented families and broke friendships. When in 1995 the immigration papers finally 'came through,' as we say in Guyana, after a decade of waiting, it was our turn to be the ones leaving. We followed the blueprint that my mother's family had mapped in their departures from Guyana. We made our way to North America to join her siblings who were now split between the US and Canada.

While witnessing the exodus of her entire family from her homeland was unbearable, nothing prepared my mother for the trials of being a new immigrant in the 1990s in the Washington, DC suburbs where we eventually settled. There she transitioned from a housewife in Guyana to a mother supporting three children on foreign soil with nothing available to her but minimum-wage jobs. When my mother got on that plane with her children and left for the unknown, did she think of her act, and the acts of what so many Guyanese and Caribbean women had done before, as brave or remarkable or necessary? Did she understand at the time how mythical the 'American Dream' was, deciding nonetheless to go after it? Was she prepared for the disappointment? What I do know for sure is that, like so many Guyanese women, my mother single-handedly rerouted the course of her children's lives, forever changing who we would become in the twenty-first-century world.

Since leaving Guyana at fourteen years old, I've now lived in the US longer than I've lived in Guyana. I am no longer confined by the term 'Resident Alien,' as my American green card first branded me. I have other labels now: Naturalized Citizen. Guyanese-American. Immigrant. I am deeply unsettled about how our global society regards the immigrant. Where some see autonomy, others see dependency. Where some see courage, others see weakness. Where some see a desire to take charge of one's destiny, others see a threat. Where some see dignity, others see failure. And at times, we are simply *not seen*. In an interview for *The Atlantic*, Haitian-American writer Edwidge Danticat poignantly steeps the *activism* of the immigrant within the poetics of an *art* practice. She writes:

> That experience of touching down in a totally foreign place is like having a blank canvas: You begin with nothing, but stroke by stroke you build a life. This process requires everything great art requires—risk-taking, hope, a great deal of imagination, all the qualities that are the building blocks of art. You must be able to dream something nearly impossible and toil to bring it into existence.[8]

Danticat's reading of the immigrant's journey as akin to art-making was inspired by a passage she read in Colombian-American Patricia Engel's memoir *It's Not Love, It's Just Paris*, in which the author's father says: 'All immigrants are artists because they create a life, a future, from nothing but a dream. The immigrant's life is art in its purest form.'[9] It is with this beautiful spirit of creativity and imagination that *Liminal Spaces: Migration and Women of the Guyanese Diaspora* gathers fifteen women of Guyanese heritage to explore their relationship to migration through the literary and visual art forms of memoir, creative non-fiction, poetry, photography, curatorial and art essays. These women are artists, activists, scholars, teachers, photographers, poets, writers, playwrights, performers, journalists, and curators. The Guyanese women whose stories are laid bare in *Liminal Spaces* reinforce Engel's notion of *the immigrant as artist*. These women remake, reinvent, and rebuild their lives, as many times as needed. Collectively they reveal that we are all, in some sense, immigrants, embarking on the constant work, the hard labor, privately and publicly, of dismantling one life to make a new one.

*

The word 'liminal,' from the Latin word *limens*, means 'threshold'—a place of transition, waiting, and unknowing. It is to be caught between worlds—one known and one to come.[10] In tandem, the title *Liminal Spaces* reflects the ways in which Guyanese women bear witness to what drives them from their homeland as well as what keeps them emotionally and psychically tethered. It is a title meant to encapsulate how they examine the notion of homeland as both fixed and unfixed, a constantly shifting idea or memory, and a physical place and psychic space.[11] *Liminal Spaces* also underscores how these women trouble and redefine ideas of migrant, immigrant, and citizen. Some directly engage with present global migration debates while avoiding the vitriol those debates are steeped in. Others challenge the labels of alien, foreigner, and outlier. Many poignantly and apolitically shine a light on the universal themes of departure, arrival, loss, up-rootedness, persistence, and faith. Collectively, the women in *Liminal Spaces* represent two spectrums of the migration arc: the ones who leave and the ones who are left. Some have stayed rooted in Guyana even as they watched their loved ones leave, year after year, for both neighboring and far-off lands. Some, although born in Guyana, maintain the rituals and traditions on the diasporic soils they now call home. Some return to Guyana often, and some rarely. Some never.

Liminal Spaces traces seven seminal decades of Guyana's history, offering a portrait of a colonial and postcolonial nation continuously evolving. The fifteen intergenerational cohort of voices range from women in their twenties to their seventies. Their personal and political histories are rooted in Guyana's multi-cultural heritages—Amerindian,

British, African, Chinese, Indian, and Portuguese. Their first-person narratives span the 1950s through present day, mirroring Guyana's journey from a British colony to an independent republic to a 'disappearing nation.'[12] For some women in this book who were born in British-ruled Guyana, bearing witness to the tumultuous birth of an independent nation and a simultaneous struggle to shirk a colonial past catalyzed their departures. The younger women, who have only known their homeland as an independent nation, still made the difficult decision to leave it. Other women who contributed to this collection have never lived in Guyana and connect only through their parents' migration narratives. As first-generation citizens of the United States, United Kingdom, and Canada, they grapple with what survives and what is mourned once their Guyanese-born parents, their direct ties to Guyana, are gone. Some of these women once lived in Guyana, and later migrated to the country's largest diasporic cities of New York, Toronto, and London. All in all, *Liminal Spaces* centers the narratives of grandmothers, mothers and daughters, immigrants and citizens—women who have labored for their country, women who are in service to a vision of what Guyanese women can and ought to be in the world.

Guyana's legacy of migration mirrors the broader emergence of Caribbean people around the globe. The narratives featured in *Liminal Spaces* counter a legacy of absence and invisibility of Guyanese women's stories. This collection—the first of its kind—is devoted entirely to the voices of women from Guyana and its expansive diaspora. Although the contributors share experiences specific to Guyana, their stories speak to migration as the defining movement of our twenty-first-century world and the tensions between place and placeless-ness, nationality and belonging, immigrant and citizen. Etched throughout the book's literary and visual narratives is the grit, agency, and artistry required of women around the world who embark on a new life in a new land or watch the ones they love do so. Within these beautiful, disruptive stories lies a simple truth: there is no single story about migration. Rather, the act of migration is infinite, full of arrivals, departures, returns, absences, and reunions.

*

One of the most defining movements of the twenty-first century is global migration. Few of us remain untouched by its sweeping narrative. In its *World Migration Report 2020*, the United Nations reported, 'The number of international migrants is estimated to be almost 272 million globally, with nearly two-thirds being labor migrants.'[13] Equally important, forty-eight percent of those migrants are women. In other words, women comprise almost half the people migrating globally.[14] As more women migrate, it means that a growing number of them are also migrating independently and becoming the breadwinners for their families. Each day, more women like my mother do whatever they need to; they board planes and boats and ships and make-shift rafts, or walk across borders, fences, and walls to carve out a better life for themselves and their families. Yet, where do we find their real stories?[15] Where is the poetry of their lives? Can we turn to art, to language, to poetry, to the image to find their voices? How can the photograph map the emotional terrain of separation from a motherland? Instead of narratives that allow us to see the real lives and dignity of these women—now in the millions—their stories of migration are often hijacked by politics, policy, sensational headlines, and data.

For the past fifty years, women have been the driving force in migration from Guyana as the UK, US, and Canada looked to the Caribbean as a source for blue collar, domestic, clerical, and healthcare workers. In 'Caribbean Migrations: The Caribbean Diaspora,' Monica Jardine writes that the pivotal role of women served as a catalytic shift in contemporary Caribbean migration:

> [I]n the Anglophone Caribbean world, in particular, modern migration became identified with women's labor and women's risk—that is, with the decision of women to internationalize their labor, to migrate alone in the first instance […] and […] to more clearly expect that their household and legal status would become more equal to that of men after migration.[16]

In 1948, the British Nationality Act gave 'full citizenship' to all people living in its commonwealth countries and full rights of entry and settlement in Britain. Throughout the 1950s and 1960s, many ambitious dreamers in then British Guiana and from other British colonies throughout the Caribbean took advantage of the 1948 Act and made their way to England.[17] They became part of what was known as the 'Windrush Generation,'[18] named after the SS Empire Windrush, the inaugural ship that brought a total of 492 Caribbean immigrants to Tilbury Dock in Essex, England on June 21, 1948. Fourteen years later, a backlash against the increasing number of the colonies' Caribbean-born workers and their families moving into Britain's neighborhoods led to the 1962 Commonwealth Immigration Act, which would overturn the Nationality Act of 1948, condemning it as an unregulated approach to immigration. Most recently, in 2018 as the British marked the 70th anniversary of the Windrush Generation, the 'Windrush Scandal' erupted leaving many Caribbean immigrants wrongly detained, denied legal rights and benefits they were entitled to as citizens, and threatened with deportation or wrongly deported from the United Kingdom.[19] In *Liminal Spaces*, contributor Maria del Pilar Kaladeen writes of the racism she endured growing up in England as a daughter of immigrants, and the pressures, including from her parents, to shirk her cultural identity to be monolithically 'British.' Born in London to a Guyanese father who was part of the notable Windrush Generation, Kaladeen shares in her essay, 'A Daughter's Journey from Indenture to Windrush,' how mythical the promises of citizenship were for those who migrated from Guyana to England. She explores the impact a vitriolic culture of racism had on Caribbean immigrants and their descendants:

> [I]f I wanted a role model in un-belonging I needn't look any further than my father—the progenitor of my incongruity. Yet everything I knew about my father's background was fragmentary. He was from a country called Guyana. It used to be a British colony. Inexplicably he was both Indian and South American. And this meant that the children who pelted the word 'Paki' at us in the streets were essentially correct. Correct in the sense that this word was used in the UK, as a derogatory term for anyone of South Asian origin.

Further, the newspaper stories of the inaugural '492 West Indian' migrants, as the British headlines boldly declared, who first arrived on England's shores via the Empire Windrush, has largely minimized the experiences of the Caribbean women who embarked on the thirty-day voyage. For example, the opening paragraph of a 1948 article, in *The Guardian*, entitled 'Why 492 West Indians Came to Britain,' leads with the question: 'What were they thinking, these 492 men [...] as the Empire Windrush slid upstream with the flood between the closing shores of Kent and Essex?'[20] In 'How Many Women Were on the Empire Windrush?' Mirko Casagranda writes:

> In its monadic and monolithic characterization, the all-inclusiveness of the figure '492' excludes women from the founding myth of arrival, as in the accounts of the time and in many subsequent recollections of the event, the passengers are homogenously defined as black male economic migrants from Jamaica, which reinforces 'a patriarchal model of travel' and enhances the stereotype of the male explorer looking for new places to settle in and form a new family as soon as *his* woman joins him in the new country.[21]

In fact, what the ship's data from the Empire Windrush passenger log does reveal is that of the 257 women aboard, 188 were traveling alone. Casagranda continues:

> It is no surprise that in the British national consciousness and collective memory of this symbolic moment, there is no space for women as they have been rather considered as a consequence, almost an appendix, of the arrival of *their* men.[22]

> [The number] '257' [...] challenges the idea of an exclusively male migration from the West Indies. [...] Although the majority of the passengers were adult males (684), these women, especially those who made the crossing alone, question the cultural assumptions of the time about gender.[23]

In the Passenger List of the Empire Windrush (Fig. I.2), the names of six British Guianese women are listed as traveling alone to England. They are summarized in the records as follows and checked under the passenger log's subcategory of 'Female' and 'Not Accompanied by Husband:'

Mary Forbes, 41 years old, 'household domestic'

Muriel Fraser, 39 years old, 'bank teller'

Edna Thompson, 32 years old, 'servant'

Phillis Teesdale, 35 years old, 'household domestic'

Ivy Wcolley, 53 years old, 'household domestic'

Marie Worley, 54 years old, 'household domestic'

The stories of Guyanese women like these from those early decades who migrated to the UK—and those of so many others who migrated later, uprooted their lives and bravely embarked on unchartered territories—remain mysteries. In a 2018 essay I wrote, titled 'Unfixed Homeland: Artists Imagining the Lives of the Guyanese Women of Windrush,' for a special issue of London's *Wasafiri Magazine* marking the 70th anniversary of the Windrush Generation, I could only pose questions about the women listed on the ship's manifest:

> How did these women end up aboard the SS Empire Windrush—travelling accompanied by neither family members nor husbands—and what were their lives like once they arrived in England? Who were these women? What were the circumstances that led to them to travel by themselves unaccompanied? What were they fleeing in British Guiana? What future were they hoping to build once they arrived in England?[25]

What happens when the archives fail us? Where do we turn when their limitations can only take us so far in excavating the lives of these women?[26] When confronted with the absences in the archives, the women writers and artists in *Liminal Spaces* must rely on their creative imaginations to tell Guyanese women's stories. The essays and poems of British-Guyanese contributors like Maria del Pilar Kaladeen and Grace Nichols reconstruct the narratives of Guyanese women in the United Kingdom and counters their invisibility in the records. Their artistic and creative imaginings echo a call to action to look beyond the archives. Their compelling work serves as a balm for the longing that still haunts many of us who want to know how these British-Guyanese women navigated an unwelcoming place and rose out of hardship to make their way.

In a similar way as in the UK, over the past five decades, Guyanese women increasingly began to make their way to the US, particularly New York City, as they saw migration as a means to improve their economic and social status and the educational opportunities of their children. The majority of the contributors featured in *Liminal Spaces* are women who live in New York City—a reflection of how the city has framed the landscape of Guyana's migration narrative. One only need walk through Flatbush and Crown Heights in Brooklyn and the Ozone Park and Richmond Hill sections of Queens (the latter affectionately known as 'Little Guyana') to witness an abundance of Guyanese 'Bake Shops' and 'Roti Shops.'[27] As the Guyanese community grew to be

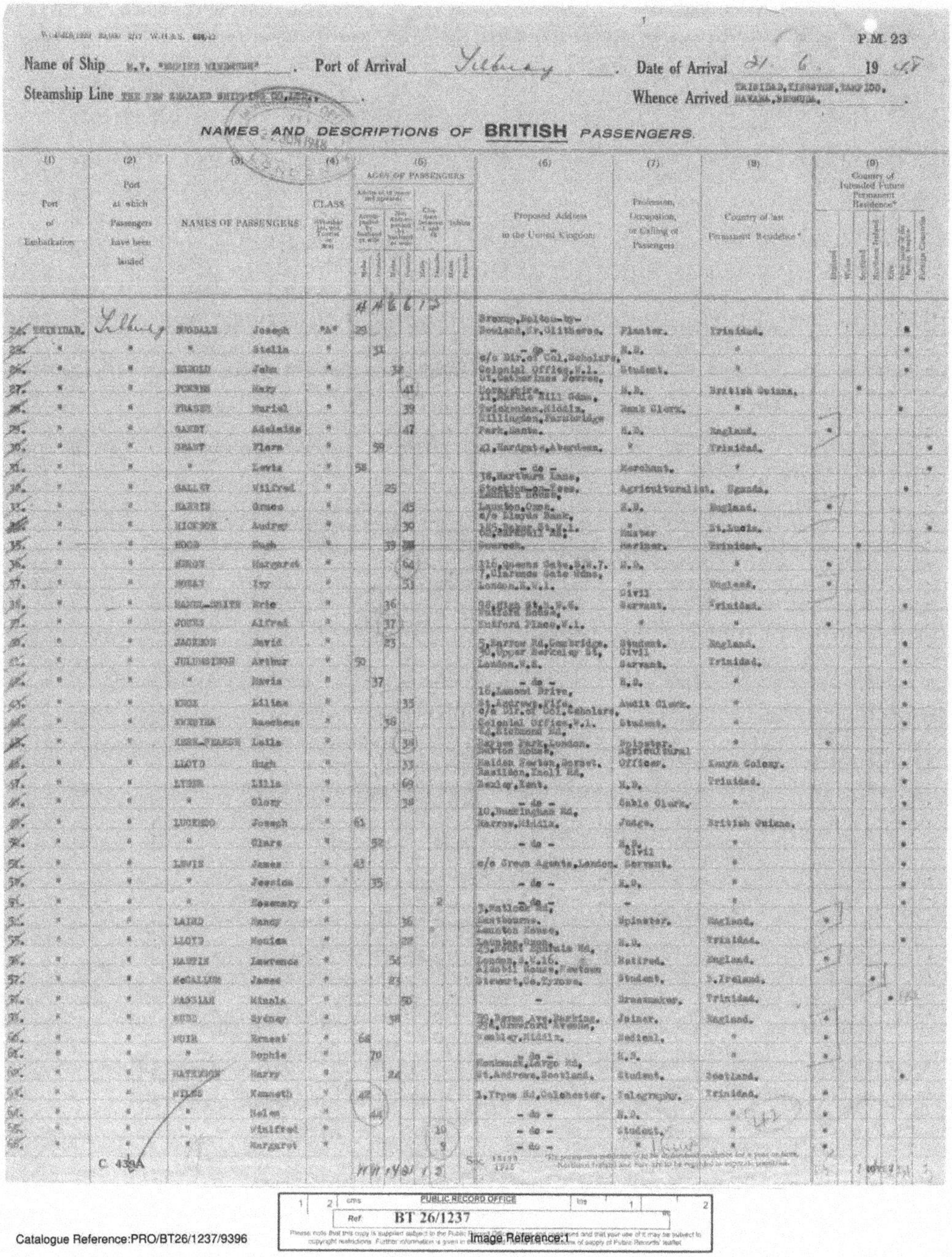
P.M. 23

Name of Ship M.V. "EMPIRE WINDRUSH". Port of Arrival Tilbury. Date of Arrival 21. 6. 1948

Steamship Line THE NEW ZEALAND SHIPPING CO., LTD. Whence Arrived TRINIDAD, KINGSTON, TAMPICO, HAVANA, BERMUDA.

NAMES AND DESCRIPTIONS OF BRITISH PASSENGERS.

(1) Port of Embarkation | (2) Port at which Passengers have been landed | (3) NAMES OF PASSENGERS | (4) CLASS | (5) AGES OF PASSENGERS | (6) Proposed Address in the United Kingdom | (7) Profession, Occupation, or Calling of Passengers | (8) Country of last Permanent Residence* | (9) Country of Intended Future Permanent Residence*

C. 439A

PUBLIC RECORD OFFICE

Ref. BT 26/1237

Image Reference:1

Catalogue Reference:PRO/BT26/1237/9396

Figure I.2

Passenger list of the SS Empire Windrush

June 1948

The National Archives, Public Domain.[24]

the fifth largest immigrant group in New York City, Guyanese women emerged to claim, 'one of the highest rates of female labor force participation among New York City immigrants.'[28] Underpaid or paid under the table, Guyanese women found jobs that were domestic in nature or in food service, healthcare, and hospitality industries. They were often part of an invisible workforce as private household workers—nannies, housekeepers, and home care aides. In *Liminal Spaces*, many essays acknowledge the Guyanese women who took on such jobs. In 'Memories from Yonder,' artist Christie Neptune features Ebora Calder who left Guyana in the 1950s as a young woman to work as a home care aide in Brooklyn, New York City where she remained until she reached retirement. In 'Concrete and Filigree,' curator Michelle Joan Wilkinson writes of her mother's arrival in the late 1960s to work in Manhattan's Garment District. And, in those first years in the late 1990s, I write in my essay 'The Geography of Separation,' about the minimum wage jobs my mother took on including as a college cafeteria server and nursing home assistant. These experiences are not unique to Guyanese women; they are a common refrain of many immigrant women in search for a better life for themselves and their families.

Along with London and New York City, the city of Toronto possesses one of the largest and oldest Guyanese populations outside of Guyana. Beginning in the mid-1950s, Guyanese became part of a larger trend of Caribbean people shifting to Canada and specifically urban cities like Toronto.[29] The West Indian Domestic Scheme (1955–1960), which allowed women from Guyana and the neighboring islands of Jamaica and Barbados to immigrate as domestic workers, paved the way for a second and larger wave of Caribbean migration in the 1970s. In her essay for *Liminal Spaces*, 'A Trace | Evidence of Time Past,' artist Sandra Brewster, who is Canadian-born, reminds us that the first Toronto Caribbean Carnival in 1967, also known as Caribana, took place during the second wave of migration to Canada. Brewster notes:

> [It] was a gesture of generosity—a gift from the Caribbean community to Canada on its 100th birthday. I see this gift as an action that permanently transferred the community's existence onto the city, creating an undeniable presence in Canadian history.

As the testament to that abiding gift, today the Toronto Caribbean Carnival is regarded as North America's largest street festival, with over one million global visitors a year. The Canadian Immigration Act (1976) further allowed more people from the Caribbean into Canada and, coupled with Canada's increased need for labor from developing nations, the Caribbean community thrived. By the early 2000s, Toronto emerged as, and remains, a prominent node in the Caribbean diaspora where Guyanese in particular are the city's third-largest Caribbean-immigrant community.

As Guyanese women continue to drive migration to the UK, US, and Canada, they have in turn ushered in a new kind agency. As early as the 1960s, Caribbean women immigrants were increasingly regarded as 'principal aliens' allowing them to sponsor visa applications for family members. In her essay, Brewster explains the pivotal role her aunt played, serving as the catalyst for bringing almost her entire family from Guyana to Canada:

> Auntie Gloria being the eldest, left Guyana first to find a place for everyone to live and to figure out the lay of the land so that when the others came she could direct them on what to do and where to do it. She was basically their orientation guide[.]

In New York City, in particular, women of the Guyanese community, more than any other immigrant group, utilize family sponsorship visas to bring members of their family to the US. However, a 2017 article in *The New York Times* reported that with the current US administration's proposed immigration policies to severely curtail family sponsorship, Guyanese women 'could lose the most from a new federal effort to cut legal immigration in half.'[30]

*

In her widely celebrated 2009 TED Talk, 'The Danger of a Single Story,' Nigerian-American author Chimamanda Ngozi Adichie shares the constant indignities of having to encounter and absorb the dangerous single story of Africa as 'a single story of catastrophe.'[31] She cautions us of the consequences when we are complicit in promoting a singular destructive narrative of a place:

> The single story creates stereotypes, and the problem with stereotypes is not that they are untrue, but that they are incomplete. They make one story become the only story [...] The consequence of the single story is this: It robs people of dignity. It makes our recognition of our equal humanity difficult. It emphasizes how we are different rather than how we are similar.[32]

Like Adiche's Nigeria, so too has Guyana been subjected to a dangerous single story rooted in catastrophe. On the world stage, Guyana has largely been portrayed in a complicated light. One need only browse the global headlines over the past fifty years. From the ethnic violence between Africans and Indians that stained Guyana's struggle for independence from the British; to the tragic Jonestown mass murder-suicide in 1978; to the revelation that by 1980, Guyana's economic situation was so dire that it was ranked as one of the poorest countries in the Western Hemisphere; to widespread political corruption during national elections in the 1990s (and currently in 2020) that required the former American president Jimmy Carter to preside; to the World Health Organization 2014 report naming Guyana as the country with the highest suicide rate in the world; to the 2017 data declaring Guyana with the highest out-migration rate in the world—the majority of the global reporting on Guyana has centered on violence, political corruption, poverty, trauma, and mass exodus. Furthermore, in the past decade, the major reporting targeting the Guyanese diasporic community abroad has been prone to negativity. Stories have focused on the lure of oil prospecting, the fragmenting effects of migration on families, political unrest, death and violence, and even unhealthy food habits. This is how the world sees and hears of Guyana. These are some of the dangerous single stories and headlines dominating international perspectives on Guyana and influencing a global understanding of who Guyanese people are.

More recently, the reporting on the promising yet tumultuous discovery of offshore oil and a chorus of viewpoints by international experts on why Guyana is 'unprepared' or too 'corrupt' or 'ill-equipped' to navigate the ensuing billion-dollar potential windfall have dominated the headlines. Notably, an extensive article in *The New York Times* in 2018 received severe backlash after its writer indulged in representations of Guyana that were dismissive and offensive. The *Times* lead paragraph in the article, 'The $20 Billion Question for Guyana,' portrayed Guyana as the impoverished tropic:

> There are a few dirt roads between villages that sit on stilts along rivers snaking through the rainforest. Children in remote areas go to school in dugout canoes, and play naked in the muggy heat.[33]

Later in the article, the reporter characterized Guyana as 'A vast watery wilderness with only three paved highways' whose economy is 'propelled by drug trafficking, money-laundering and gold and diamond smuggling.'[34] The Guyanese diaspora united in an uproar against this reductive characterization. Dr. Oneka LaBennett, Guyanese-American scholar and professor, harshly critiqued the portrayal, writing on Twitter:

> Misrepresenting Guyana as a place 'forgotten by time' where children 'play naked in the muggy heat' denies its complexity. Dangerous distortions like this inform the perilous trajectory of my homeland's oil boom. Do better @nytimes.[35]

Guyana, like all nations, is a complicated place with its unique struggles. Nevertheless, it remains a beloved homeland for many of its citizens and those in its wide diaspora across the Caribbean, North America and Europe. The spotlight will continue to grow on Guyana as its future is now entangled with oil production. The world is now invested in how things play out in what the media is already framing as Guyana's 'rags to riches' story. Yet, it continues to be a global malpractice that the majority of the stories told about us, are not by us, which in itself is its own kind of unique danger. Furthermore, as the 2018 *New York Times* article reflected, what the global public often sees of the visual culture of Guyana still centers on the exotic, tropical, colonial, and touristic. In response, the artists and writers in *Liminal Spaces* are part of a contemporary movement to challenge and disrupt the reductive narratives often associated with the region. While the fifteen contributors in *Liminal Spaces* are honest about the hard truths of a country grappling with violence, poverty, and constant departure, they simultaneously offer, eloquently and unabashedly, restorative narratives of their homeland. In doing so, we see the persistent role of women in countering the dangerous single stories of Guyana through their first-person narratives and their art-making.

Chapters

L iminal Spaces: Migration and Women of the Guyanese Diaspora is organized into four parts: 'Part I: Mothering Lands,' 'Part II: The Ones Who Leave . . . The Ones Who Are Left,' 'Part III: Transitions,' and 'Part IV: Returns, Reunions, and Rituals.' Conceived as a visual exhibition on the page, the fifteen contributors' essays and artworks are curated as a four-part journey—one that allows the reader to trace the migration path of Guyanese women from their motherlands, to their moment of departure, to their arrival on diasporic soils, to their reunion with Guyana, and all that flows in between.

'Part I: Mothering Lands' engages the tensions between *motherland*, the place of birth; and *otherland*, the space of othering. The essays take us through the voyages undertaken by mothers born in Guyana and their daughters born in the diaspora. Artists Keisha Scarville (United States) and Erika DeFreitas (Canada) and journalist Natalie Hopkinson with her mother Serena Hopkinson (Canada/United States) reveal how their mother-daughter relationships serve as a metaphor for their relationship with Guyana—a space frequently wrestled with as a mythical motherland. As they reflect on their immigrant mothers' journeys, their gaze as daughters is full of compassion and tenderness.

In Part II, there are two spectrums of the migration arc: the ones who leave and the ones who are left. Yet, too often the narratives of the latter are constantly eclipsed. 'The Ones Who Leave . . . The Ones Who Are Left' counters the discourse and creative representations on migration that are overwhelmingly focused on the ones who leave. Through travelogue, memoir, art, and photography essays, I, Grace Aneiza Ali (United States), Dominique Hunter (Guyana), Khadija Benn (Guyana), and Ingrid Griffith (United States), center the stories of those who remain.

'Part III: Transitions' explores how Guyanese women unfold a life in a past land to construct a life in a new land; how they are made, unmade, and remade again. Poet Grace Nichols (United Kingdom) and visual artists Suchitra Mattai (United States), Christie Neptune (United States), and Sandra Brewster (Canada), detail the transition from citizen to immigrant. Their stories implore us to ponder: How do we hold steadfast to our dreams, when in order to survive we must diminish parts of the self? Revealed throughout these essays is a commitment to use their artistic practices as spaces for Guyanese women to speak, to be heard, and to be seen.

For those of us who have left one country for another, how do we return and how do we stay connected? What tangible things do we cling to? In 'Part IV: Returns, Reunions, and Rituals,' Michelle Joan Wilkinson (United States), Maria del Pilar Kaladeen (United Kingdom), and Maya Mackrandilal (United States) write about their returns to Guyana and the ways in which they are tethered to the houses, lands, and sacred heirlooms embedded within their family legacies. They explore how daughters of immigrants rekindle, restore, and repair frayed bonds and illuminate how we lose, rediscover, and reunite with a place.

While, the voices of Guyanese women remain under-the-radar in literature, the women in *Liminal Spaces* are shining ambassadors of Guyana's multiple stories. Our literary and artistic practices function as declarations that the women of Guyana will not disappear into history. What bonds us is a profound love for Guyana. With that love comes responsibility. What does it mean to love a place? How do we express that love, especially if we no longer live there? What is our accountability to this place? As I've poured over the work of these Guyanese women with multiple hats on—curator, editor, daughter of Guyana, immigrant—I see love embedded in the essays and art so generously offered throughout the pages of *Liminal Spaces*. I am moved by their brilliance and innovation, by the thoughtful and provocative conversations and challenging and disruptive questions their work allows us to have. We remain ever so grateful for a homeland that continues to shape all of our lives.

Bibliography

Adichie, Chimamanda Ngozi, 'The Danger of a Single Story,' filmed July 2009 in Oxford, United Kingdom, TED video, 18:34, https://www.ted.com/talks/chimamanda_ngozi_adichie_the_danger_of_a_single_story

Ali, Grace Aneiza, *Liminal Space*, curated by Grace Aneiza Ali, Caribbean Cultural Center African Diaspora Institute (New York), 17 June 2017–30 November 2017, https://artsandculture.google.com/culturalinstitute/beta/exhibit/liminal-space-cccadi/GgJy2wYqU_fXJA?hl=en

Ali, Grace Aneiza, *Un | Fixed Homeland*, curated by Grace Aneiza Ali, Aljira, a Center for Contemporary Art (Newark, NJ), 17 July 2016–23 September 2016, https://view.joomag.com/un-fixed-homeland-aljira-center-for-contemporary-art-2016-catalog-un-fixed-homeland/0430951001481910086

Ali, Grace Aneiza, 'Unfixed Homeland: Artists Imagining the Lives of the Guyanese Women of Windrush,' *Wasafiri Magazine*, 33/2 (2018), 31–40, https://doi.org/10.1080/02690055.2018.1433272

Barron, Carrie, 'Creativity and the Liminal Space,' *Psychology Today*, 4 June 2013, https://www.psychologytoday.com/us/blog/the-creativity-cure/201306/creativity-and-the-liminal-space

Casagranda, Mirko, 'How Many Women Were on the Empire Windrush? Regendering Black British Culture in Andrea Levy's *Small Island*,' *Textus*, 23/2 (2010), 355–370.

Central Intelligence Agency, *The CIA World Factbook 2017*, https://www.cia.gov/library/publications/the-world-factbook/geos/gy.html

Dabydeen, David, 'A Disappearing Nation,' *Neither There Nor Here*, BBC Radio 4, 28 February 2017, http://www.bbc.co.uk/programmes/b08gmtx1

Engel, Patricia, *It's Not Love, It's Just Paris* (New York: Grove Press, 2013).

Fassler, Joe, 'All Immigrants Are Artists,' *The Atlantic*, 27 August 2013, https://www.theatlantic.com/entertainment/archive/2013/08/all-immigrants-are-artists/279087/

Jardine, Monica, 'Caribbean Migrations: The Caribbean Diaspora,' in *Encyclopedia of the African Diaspora: Origins, Experiences, and Culture*, ed. by Carole Boyce Davies (Santa Barbara: ABC-CLIO, 2008), pp. 270– 285.

Krauss, Clifford, 'The $20 Billion Question for Guyana,' *The New York Times*, 20 July 2018, https://www.nytimes.com/2018/07/20/business/energy-environment/the-20-billion-question-for-guyana.html

McAuliffe, Marie, and Binod Khadria, *World Migration Report 2020* (Geneva: United Nations International Organization for Migration, 2019), https://www.un.org/sites/un2.un.org/files/wmr_2020.pdf

Nasta, Susheila, ed., 'Windrush Women,' *Wasafiri Magazine*, 33/2 (2018), 1–2, https://doi.org/10.1080/02690055.2018.1437196

New York City's Mayor's Office of Immigrant Affairs (MOIA), *The State of Our Immigrant City, Annual Report 2020*, https://www1.nyc.gov/site/immigrants/about/annual-report.page

'No Passport Required: Queens, NYC,' *PBS*, 31 July 2018, https://www.pbs.org/video/queens-nyc-ixejwj/

Rodgers, Lucy, and Maryam Ahmed, 'Windrush: Who Exactly Was on Board?,' *BBC News*, 21 June 2019, https://www.bbc.com/news/uk-43808007

Semple, Kirk, 'Take the A Train to Little Guyana,' *The New York Times*, 8 June 2013, http://archive.nytimes.com/www.nytimes.com/interactive/2013/06/09/nyregion/new-york-citys-newest-immigrant-enclaves.html

Serhan, Yasmeen, 'When Even Legal Residents Face Deportation,' *The Atlantic*, 19 April 2018, https://www.theatlantic.com/international/archive/2018/04/windrush-generation-uk-facing-deportation/558317/

Smith, Zadie, *White Teeth* (New York: Vintage International, 2000).

Special Correspondent, 'Why 492 West Indians came to Britain,' *The Guardian*, 23 June 1948, https://www.theguardian.com/century/1940-1949/Story/0,,105104,00.html

Vidal, Elisa Mosler, and Jasper Dag Tjaden, *Global Migration Indicators, 2018* (Berlin: Global Migration Data Analysis Centre (GMDAC) and United Nations International Organization for Migration, 2018), https://publications.iom.int/system/files/pdf/global_migration_indicators_2018.pdf

United Nations, Department of Economic and Social Affairs, Population Division, *World Population Prospects 2019, Online Edition. Rev. 1.*, https://population.un.org/wpp/Download/Standard/Population/

Wang, Vivian, 'In Little Guyana, Proposed Cuts to Family Immigration Weigh Heavily,' *The New York Times*, 11 August 2017, https://www.nytimes.com/2017/08/11/nyregion/in-little-guyana-proposed-cuts-to-family-immigration-weigh-heavily.html

Endnotes

1. Epigraph from 'Five Measures of Expatriation: III Going Nowhere, Getting Somewhere,' in *Measures of Expatriation* (Manchester: Carcanet Press, 2016), p. 100. Used by courtesy of Vahni Capildeo.

2. New York City's Mayor's Office of Immigrant Affairs (MOIA), *The State of Our Immigrant City*, *Annual Report 2020*, p. 16, https://www1.nyc.gov/site/immigrants/about/annual-report.page

3. United Nations, Department of Economic and Social Affairs, Population Division, *World Population Prospects 2019, Online Edition. Rev. 1*, https://population.un.org/wpp/Download/Standard/Population/

4. Guyana's emigration rate is among the highest in the world; more than 55% of its citizens reside abroad. Central Intelligence Agency, *The CIA World Factbook 2017*, https://www.cia.gov/library/publications/the-world-factbook/geos/gy.html

5. For more information, see 'Postface: A Brief History of Migration from Guyana.'

6. David Dabydeen, 'A Disappearing Nation,' *Neither There Nor Here*, BBC Radio 4, 28 February 2017, http://www.bbc.co.uk/programmes/b08gmtx1

7. Zadie Smith, *White Teeth* (New York: Vintage International, 2000), p. 461.

8. Joe Fassler, 'All Immigrants Are Artists,' *The Atlantic*, 27 August 2013, https://www.theatlantic.com/entertainment/archive/2013/08/all-immigrants-are-artists/279087/

9. Patricia Engel, *It's Not Love, It's Just Paris* (New York: Grove Press, 2013).

10. Although the term has varied meanings in the fields of theology, psychology, anthropology, and art, I am drawn to Richard Rohr's theological definition, which frames 'liminal' as a journey in which one place is left for another. He notes: 'It is when you have left the tried and true but have not yet been able to replace it with anything else. It is when you are between your old comfort zone and any possible new answer.' Cited in Carrie Barron, 'Creativity and the Liminal Space,' *Psychology Today*, June 4, 2013, https://www.psychologytoday.com/us/blog/the-creativity-cure/201306/creativity-and-the-liminal-space

11. This book project has been informed and inspired by two exhibitions I curated featuring Guyanese artists and their relationship to art, migration, and the idea of the 'liminal:' *Un | Fixed Homeland*, curated by Grace Aneiza Ali, Aljira, a Center for Contemporary Art (Newark, NJ), 17 July 2016–23 September 2016, https://view.joomag.com/un-fixed-homeland-aljira-center-for-contemporary-art-2016-catalog-un-fixed-homeland/0430951001481910086; and *Liminal Space*, curated by Grace Aneiza Ali, Caribbean Cultural Center African Diaspora Institute (New York), 17 June 2017–30 November 2017, https://artsandculture.google.com/culturalinstitute/beta/exhibit/liminal-space-cccadi/GgJy2wYqU_fXJA?hl=en

12. See Dabydeen, 'A Disappearing Nation.'

13. Marie McAuliffe and Binod Khadria, *World Migration Report 2020* (Geneva: United Nations International Organization for Migration, 2019), p. 2, https://www.un.org/sites/un2.un.org/files/wmr_2020.pdf

14. Elisa Mosler Vidal and Jasper Dag Tjaden, *Global Migration Indicators, 2018* (Berlin: Global Migration Data Analysis Centre (GMDAC) and United Nations International Organization for Migration, 2018), https://publications.iom.int/system/files/pdf/global_migration_indicators_2018.pdf

15. See *Women and Migration: Responses in Art and History*, ed. by Deborah Willis, Ellyn Toscano, and Kalia Brooks Nelson (Cambridge: Open Book Publishers, 2019) for a range of essays charting how women around the globe have articulated their experiences of migration in writing, photography, art, and film. I was honored to contribute Chapter 36, 'The Ones Who Leave . . . the Ones Who Are Left: Guyanese Migration Story,' pp. 473–489.

16. Monica Jardine, 'Caribbean Migrations: The Caribbean Diaspora,' in *Encyclopedia of the African Diaspora: Origins, Experiences, and Culture*, ed. by Carole Boyce Davies (Santa Barbara: ABC-CLIO, 2008), pp. 270–285 (pp. 277–278).

17. For more information, see 'Postface: A Brief History of Migration from Guyana.'

18. Lucy Rodgers and Maryam Ahmed, 'Windrush: Who Exactly Was on Board?,' *BBC News*, 21 June 2019, https://www.bbc.com/news/uk-43808007

19. Yasmeen Serhan, 'When Even Legal Residents Face Deportation,' *The Atlantic*, 19 April 2018, https://www.theatlantic.com/international/archive/2018/04/windrush-generation-uk-facing-deportation/558317/

20. Special Correspondent, 'Why 492 West Indians Came to Britain,' *The Guardian*, 23 June 1948, https://www.theguardian.com/century/1940-1949/Story/0,,105104,00.html

21. Mirko Casagranda, 'How Many Women Were on the Empire Windrush? Regendering Black British Culture in Andrea Levy's *Small Island*,' *Textus*, 23/2 (2010), 355–370 (p. 357).

22. The number 257 includes every woman above the age of twelve and those accompanied by their husband (69) and those travelling alone (188). Out of these 257 women, 203 were British subjects, which included every British citizen who also lived in the colonies and territories. Casagranda, 'How Many Women,' pp. 357–358.

23. Casagranda, 'How Many Women,' p. 358.

24. Passenger List of the EMPIRE WINDRUSH, June 1948, The National Archives, Reference: BT 26/1237/9396. Selected passenger logs and historical details can be found online, http://www.movinghere.org.uk//galleries/histories/caribbean/journeys/journeys.htm#after_windrush

25. Grace Aneiza Ali, 'Unfixed Homeland: Artists Imagining the Lives of the Guyanese Women of Windrush,' *Wasafiri Magazine*, 33/2 (2018), 31–40 (p. 34), https://doi.org/10.1080/02690055.2018.1433272

26. For more on the Women of Windrush see Sushelia Nasta, ed., 'Windrush Women,' *Wasafiri Magazine*, 33/2 (2018), 1–2, https://doi.org/10.1080/02690055.2018.1437196

27. New York City has begun to take note of the contributions of our small but mighty community. In 2018, *PBS* dedicated an entire episode of its series, *No Passport Required*, to the Guyanese immigrant community in Queens. 'No Passport Required: Queens, NYC,' *PBS*, 31 July 2018, https://www.pbs.org/video/queens-nyc-ixejwj/. See also Kirk Semple, 'Take the A Train to Little Guyana,' *The New York Times*, 8 June 2013, http://archive.nytimes.com/www.nytimes.com/interactive/2013/06/09/nyregion/new-york-citys-newest-immigrant-enclaves.html

28. Vivian Wang, 'In Little Guyana, Proposed Cuts to Family Immigration Weigh Heavily,' The New York Times, 11 August 2017, https://www.nytimes.com/2017/08/11/nyregion/in-little-guyana-proposed-cuts-to-family-immigration-weigh-heavily.html

29. For more information, see 'Postface: A Brief History of Migration from Guyana.'

30. 'The Guyanese community brings in more people through family preference visas than any other immigrant group in the city.' Wang, 'In Little Guyana.'

31. Chimamanda Ngozi Adichie, 'The Danger of a Single Story,' filmed July 2009 in Oxford, United Kingdom, TED video, 18:34, https://www.ted.com/talks/chimamanda_ngozi_adichie_the_danger_of_a_single_story

32. Ibid.

33. Clifford Krauss, 'The $20 Billion Question for Guyana,' *The New York Times*, 20 July 2018, https://www.nytimes.com/2018/07/20/business/energy-environment/the-20-billion-question-for-guyana.html

34. Ibid.

35. Oneka LaBennett, 20 July 2018, https://twitter.com/OnekaLaBennett/status/1020282351392362504

About the Art, Photography, and Curatorial Notes

Liminal Spaces is a visual feast of the art and photography of migration. Many of the contributors are contemporary visual artists who accompany their essays with compelling bodies of work informed by their unique experiences of migration. This collection is also teeming with photographs from the contributors' personal collections: treasured and sacredly guarded images—family albums, archival images of British Guiana, contemporary photography on Guyana, passport photos, and scans of letters.

As the editor of this collection, I turned to my curatorial practice as a blueprint for its organization. Instead of walls, I conceived *Liminal Spaces* as a visual exhibition on the page. I open Parts I, II, III, and IV with 'curatorial notes' on each Chapter. They are meant to serve as brief introductions and to provide biographical and historical context where needed. They are invitations to the reader to delve deeper into the essays, poems, photography, and art. These curatorial notes are culled from my collaborations with the contributors, correspondences and conversations between us that have unfolded over a period of time, exhibitions I've curated, and my published writings on their work.

—Grace Aneiza Ali

PART I

MOTHERING LANDS

The mother's body is the country
of our earliest memory, the soil
from which we are formed.
Our lives are an arc of flight:
away, toward, away.

Shara McCallum, 'From the Book of Mothers'[1]

Mothering Lands engages the tensions between our place of birth (*motherland*) and the space of othering (*otherland*). For artists Keisha Scarville (United States), Erika DeFreitas (Canada), and journalist Natalie Hopkinson (Canada/United States), all first-generation daughters, their relationships with their Guyanese-born mothers serve as a metaphor for their relationship with Guyana—a space frequently wrestled with as a mythical motherland. They illustrate how their mothers, grandmothers, great grandmothers, and oldest mothers are their deepest and most tangible connection to their ancestral land. As they reflect on their immigrant mothers' journeys across Guyana, the US, and Canada, their gaze as daughters is full of compassion and tenderness. They each mine their family archives—photo albums, letters, clothing, oral stories, sacred rituals, and recipes—to shepherd us through multiple migrations and returns.

Artist **Keisha Scarville** spent her childhood raised in Brooklyn where her parents, along with so many other Guyanese immigrants, migrated and settled after leaving Guyana in the 1960s. In her photography essay, 'Surrogate Skin: Portrait of Mother (Land),' Scarville reflects on her portraiture series, 'Mama's Clothes,' an homage to her late mother. In the portraits, Scarville embodies her mother's dresses to evoke her connection to Guyana. In both her prose and portraits, Scarville grounds herself in her mother's place of birth of Buxton (Guyana) and her neighborhood of Flatbush (US). The lush, organic landscapes in these images, shifting between Guyana and the US, hold emotional and geographical significance: they capture the artist and her mother's dance between transient spaces. Grappling with 'a sense of displacement and an internal fracturing' after her mother's passing, Scarville looked to her 'mama's clothes' of bright colors, strong prints, and long flowing fabrics for meaning. She drapes and layers her body in her mother's clothing as well as fashions masks and veils to cover her face, which is always obscured. In merging her body with her mother's

 https://doi.org/10.11647/OBP.0218.01

clothes, Scarville marries both time and space—two generations, two homelands, and the complexities in between.

In an artistic practice steeped in process, gesture, performance, and documentation, Canadian-born artist **Erika DeFreitas** generously mines her family archive of photographs and letters throughout her oeuvre. In her art essay, 'Until I Hear from You,' she turns to old letters and photos sent from Guyana to construct memories with a grandmother she's never met and to piece together a motherland she's never known. Her grandmother, a skilled baker in British Guiana in the 1950s, passed down the practice to DeFreitas' mother who then migrated to Canada in 1970. In sharing her family album, DeFreitas illustrates how the act of passing on sacred crafts through two geographies and three generations of DeFreitas women has shaped her connection to Guyana. In her essay, she expands on how she uses cake icing—perfected so beautifully by her grandmother that she taught classes in cake décor to the women in her neighborhood—as an important symbol in her work as well as in her poetic language. The icing is both material and process—meant to decorate and to preserve. DeFreitas leaves us to ponder the question: Even when we commit to preserving a motherland's memories, rites, and traditions, how do we navigate the inevitable loss that pervades?

In a series of letters that read as intimate journal entries, letters that could easily belong to familiar collections like 'Letters to My Younger Self,' letters that unveil deep untold secrets and desires, mother and daughter **Serena Hopkinson** and **Natalie Hopkinson** reveal the great love and admiration that abides at the core of their relationship. It is a mother-daughter bond that has seen several migrations across three countries: Guyana, Canada, the US, and many returns and reunions in between. Guyanese-born Serena Hopkinson migrated to Toronto in 1970 as a young bride who would soon embark on building a family of her own while navigating the terrain of being an immigrant in Canada and later the United States. The Hopkinson family life was one in constant transition, defined as being 'on the move.' The letters the Hopkinson women write to each other in 'Electric Dreams' are symbolic postmarks of the places they have borne witness to, survived, and thrived: Pomeroon River, Guyana; Edmonton, Canada; and Florida and Washington, DC, United States. Like so many immigrant families who have left Guyana, a series of arrivals and departures in search of 'a better life,' took its toll on Serena's marriage and on Natalie, her Canadian-born daughter's identity and selfhood. What this duo brings to light is that despite the emotional toll migration takes on families, their relationship has been a constant driving force. It continues, to this day, to sustain, inspire, and buoy them as they chart new paths and adventures in their roles as women, daughters, wives, mothers, grandmothers, teachers and life-long learners.

While they share the great losses within their maternal histories, revealing how migration, death, and loss are inextricably linked, Scarville, DeFreitas, and Natalie and

Serena Hopkinson unpack how Guyana continues to be a land that mothers. Their essays in *Mothering Lands* are poignant examples of how as daughters of Guyana we can reach to and rely on our mothers as constant collaborators and co-authors in both our lives and in our art.

Notes

1. Epigraph from 'The Book of Mothers' in *This Strange Land*. Copyright © 2010, 2011 by Shara McCallum. Reprinted with the permission of The Permissions Company, LLC on behalf of the author and Alice James Books, www.alicejamesbooks.org

1.

Surrogate Skin: Portrait of Mother (Land)

—

Keisha Scarville

Figure 1.1
Keisha Scarville, 'After (Mom and Me)'
2015, watercolor in archival inkjet print.

    https://doi.org/10.11647/OBP.0218.02

My mother stands in the front yard of my grandfather's house in Buxton. The soft morning rain soaks through her nightgown. The weight of the water compels the thin pink fabric to cling to the fullness of her skin. It's been ten years since my mother's feet have touched the fleshy soil of this land.

If only time could unfold the labyrinth of the history of this land—before the rumors and crime, before my mother was a little girl coming home for her noon day lunch, before my grandfather looked at my grandmother, claiming her sixteen-year-old body as his woman. If only my mother could touch rock and sand to see into the past to when this place was once an abandoned plantation called New Orange Nassau. If only she could see how it forged a new center of existence, purchased in 1840 by 128 emancipated Africans who renamed it in honor of the British Parliamentarian who advocated for the gradual liberation of African slaves—Thomas Buxton.[1]

Now my mother has returned, positioning herself near the slowly dying tamarind tree that my grandfather used to climb, about a quarter mile away from the endless sea wall, and just a few yards from the upstairs bedroom where my grandfather quietly closed his eyes to this world for good. The air is different and familiar, filled with the smell of freshly cleansed leaves, sweet saltwater, and the faint sound of crowing. My mother closes her eyes and raises her face to the pouring sky. My aunt yells out to her, but she does not respond. She lifts her hands, rubs the rain deeper into her skin and smooths the silken water like lotion over her body. The words that come out of my mother's mouth are indecipherable. I sit tightly packed on the worn wooden steps and bear witness to this ad hoc baptism. Slowly my mother walks back to the elevated house. Each footstep leaves a moist trace of her hardened soles. As she gets closer, I focus on the drips of water collecting like beads on her feet. I am transfixed. This is the last time my mother and I would be together in Guyana. In a few hours, the sun will push its way through the clouds, transforming all of this into a dry landscape of memory.

My mother left Guyana in 1967. She was the oldest of five and the first in her family to travel to the United States. Her motivations for leaving Guyana were an unequivocal certainty. 'I had to leave,' she would say when reflecting on that moment in her life. 'I couldn't stay.' My mother was one of many Guyanese citizens who left during the late sixties, driven by a promise of opportunity and a new narrative to be unearthed within foreign landscapes. My father and several friends preceded her arrival. Though my mother chose to emigrate to the US, she maintained a connection to the land of her birth, firmly planting one foot under a tamarind tree in Buxton and the other, rooted on the rooftop of an apartment building in Flatbush, Brooklyn, New York. When I was a child, Guyana was a place that existed partly in my imagination and partly in my memory—stitched together like patchwork by what my parents carried with them and reassembled here in America, and my own experiences during short visits to see my family who remained. However, as the years went by, those visits became less frequent and Guyana lived mostly within my mind as a growing myth of what I regarded as a form of home and motherland.

On 13 August 2015, my mother passed away, taking with her a treasure chest of stories and deep knowing. Like how to properly clap a roti skin, or how to speak the vegetal language of soil and plant life, or how to clean and prepare your house so that good luck will come in the new year. In the months leading up to her passing, we often talked about the idea of home. I wondered whether she would ever return to Guyana. Or, like so many immigrants who moved to the States, let time and distance alter her relationship to the land. Did she now consider America her permanent home? In recounting her experiences when she arrived in the US, she often discussed the first sensation of real cold, the strange taste of American chicken, and overcoming the embedded alienation of this place.

I became curious as to how my mother's presence within this American landscape influenced her sense of belonging. How had the process of becoming an American citizen affected her? What was the impact of her shifting relationship to Guyana? Even now, I find myself left with more questions than answers.

The death of my mother left me with a sense of displacement and an internal fracturing. Her friends, most of whom also made the journey from Guyana to plant seeds in the US, would comfort me by saying, 'Alma is going home.' The word *home* became both a troubled and expansive concept—more amorphous than concrete. I started to realize that an element I regarded as home—my mother's body—was now missing. In her place were all that she accumulated as an American.

I was inundated with remnants of her existence, specifically her clothing. My mother's closets overflowed with bright colors, strong prints, and long flowing fabrics. When I was a little girl, I would often play dress up in my mother's clothes and imagine the day I would fill her dresses and assert my body as a woman. Her clothes would hang off my small skinny frame, loosely encasing all my prepubescent delights and aspirations. I reveled in this form of role-playing. I found both amusement and comfort in my mother's clothes, where her scent seemed to linger and cling to each fiber.

As an homage to my mother, I decided to photograph myself in her clothes. I wanted to find a way to ease the anxiety of separation by conjuring her presence within the photographic realm. I allowed the assemblage of clothes to drip off my body as though it were a residual, surrogate skin.

Figure 1.2
Keisha Scarville, 'Untitled #2'

from the series, 'Mama's Clothes', 2015, archival digital inkjet print.

Transient borders and undulating lands speak of histories that have long past. I stood on the shores of a beach in New York and looked out to see myself walking along the Sea Wall in Guyana.

Figure 1.3
Keisha Scarville, 'Untitled #1'

from the series, 'Mama's Clothes', 2015, archival digital inkjet print.

Figure 1.4
Keisha Scarville, 'Untitled #3'

from the series, 'Mama's Clothes', 2015, archival digital inkjet print.

Beneath the weight of her clothes, I exist as beneath a veil. I breathe my mother into me and feel her presence in my body.

Figure 1.5
Keisha Scarville, 'Veil #1'
from the series, 'Mama's Clothes', 2015, archival digital inkjet print.

Absence is a space filled with desire. I became interested in the experience of absence and the camera's role in visualizing that which cannot be seen but felt.

Figure 1.6
Keisha Scarville, 'Veil #2'
from the series, 'Mama's Clothes', 2016, archival digital inkjet print.

The presence of the landscape became an important factor in the images I created. I chose locations that held emotional and geographical significance to be read as echoes of my mother's body. In early 2016, I returned to Guyana—this time alone. I chose to investigate the terrain from a different point of view—a first-generation American-daughter searching for home. I wanted to peel back the ancestral layers and examine my own sense of belonging. I brought a suitcase of my mother's clothes and returned to Buxton. I photographed myself in and around my grandfather's house and along the Sea Wall. It was a process of repositioning and reconstitution for both my mother and myself.

Figure 1.7
Keisha Scarville, 'Untitled #5'

from the series, 'Mama's Clothes', 2016, archival digital inkjet print.

Figure 1.8
Keisha Scarville, 'Untitled #4'

from the series, 'Mama's Clothes', 2016, archival digital inkjet print.

Figure 1.9
Keisha Scarville, 'Untitled #8'
from the series, 'Mama's Clothes', 2016, archival digital inkjet print.

I often think about why my mother chose to bathe herself in the rain that day. I wondered what it meant for her to return and how her identity became subjected to shifting landscapes. I tried to find the place where my mother stood that day, but the ground was not the same. I cannot cleanse myself of the loss I experienced. I can only find a new name for a new place and for a new body.

Notes

1. 'Buxton, Rich in African Cultures,' *Kaieteur News*, 1 August 2016, https://www.kaieteurnewsonline.com/2016/08/01/buxton-rich-in-african-cultures/

2.

Until I Hear from You

—

Erika DeFreitas

Figure 2.1

My mother Cita DeFreitas and grandmother Angela DeFreitas (nèe Vieira) in their home in Georgetown, Guyana, then British Guiana, ca. 1965.

https://doi.org/10.11647/OBP.0218.03

On Imagined Geographies

My mother, Cita DeFreitas, was born in her family home in Alberttown, Georgetown, British Guiana on 10 December 1951. She was the youngest of three siblings. She left Guyana for Toronto, Canada in July 1970, citing political and economic reasons for her departure. She was eighteen years old. She left with two hundred dollars, one suitcase filled with clothes, and a small off-white carry-on just big enough to carry her tiny pillow and the only doll she ever owned.

You're growing up in a country as a young girl [where]
there wasn't much opportunity [...] It's hard to even imagine
my mother letting me go, at that age, as a young girl, growing
up in a sheltered life.[1]

She returned ten years later with me in tow a month after my birth in 1980, when her mother, Angela DeFreitas (nèe Vieira) lay in a comatose state between white sheets. What she remembers is what I remember. It is all fragmented and disjointed and pieced together in ways that may or may not make sense to those who are living in the land in the present. What I remember of these geographies can be found in a particular set of ink drawn landscapes that were mass produced in Guyana. They are framed and hang on a bathroom wall in our home. They, too, have migrated. My grandfather, Carlos DeFreitas, co-owned a store on Holmes Street that framed paintings in wooden frames. My mother lived on First Street, moved to DaSilva Street, then to Hadfield Street, and to Cowan Street—in homes that housed up to seven people at times.

From my mother, I heard of Stabroek Market, Kaieteur Falls, and jungles where large snakes traveled in pairs. I heard of homes that stood on stilts. My mother talks about back home but has never been back since her own mother's passing in 1980. She does not want to see how it all has changed. Change changing changes. It must be better than having to stand in line for a loaf of bread. Rations: cheese, milk, flour, and sugar. Yet, no matter how hard one may try, some things just don't change. Like the cadence in her speech, how pepper becomes peppa and daughter becomes daughta. This is how I know that we both imagine.

Figure 2.2

A portrait of my grandmother Angela taken in British Guiana (year unknown).

Figure 2.3

My mother Cita in front of her house on Hadfield Street, Georgetown, Guyana, ca. 1965.

On Migration

These notes written over the course of three years, between 8 November 1973 and 15 October 1976, in cursive, have crossed borders and exchanged hands. They were written by my grandmother to my mother after she left Guyana. These sentences, extracted from several letters (Fig. 2.4), have been examined and rearranged by me.

Just a few lines to let you know, we are all o.k. I am told it is getting very cold. Don't worry, I will keep you posted, remember you are as near to me as the phone. I hope you get your passport soon. Things are just the same here, with a few more shortages every now and then but we can get by somehow. I have not heard from you since my last letter, I hope you are well. Just a few lines to let you know both dad and I are still alive. I myself had to see the doctor on Monday before you phoned. Dad wants you to apply to immigration for himself and me, I know this is going to be a surprise, but he has finally decided to make a move. But on Saturday morning I began to feel faint again so I decided to see the doctor and of course he ordered me to the hospital right away as he suspected I had a slight heart attack. Everything is just as you left it, only for some robberies at a few pawn shops and jewelry shops with masked bandits with guns, cutlasses, and knives. Plenty of rain is still falling, and now we expect to have high tides next week, so everybody is preparing for floods. I dreamt last night of you and I had a feeling I would have heard from you. I am working on a wedding cake for Saturday. I had it framed and have it on my glass cabinet, so that you are looking over everything that goes on in the house. Everything around this time as you would know is centered around Mashramani, the tenth anniversary of Independence. Let me know if you need anything in particular, besides pepper sauce, guava cheese, guava jelly, cassareep, and thyme. I am sending you two pairs of slippers, a bottle of pepper sauce, some dried sorrel, and some thyme. I am moving from there and I am going to live on Murray Street out very far from where I am. About your invitation to dad, nothing doing, he says you can come home instead. Until I hear from you.

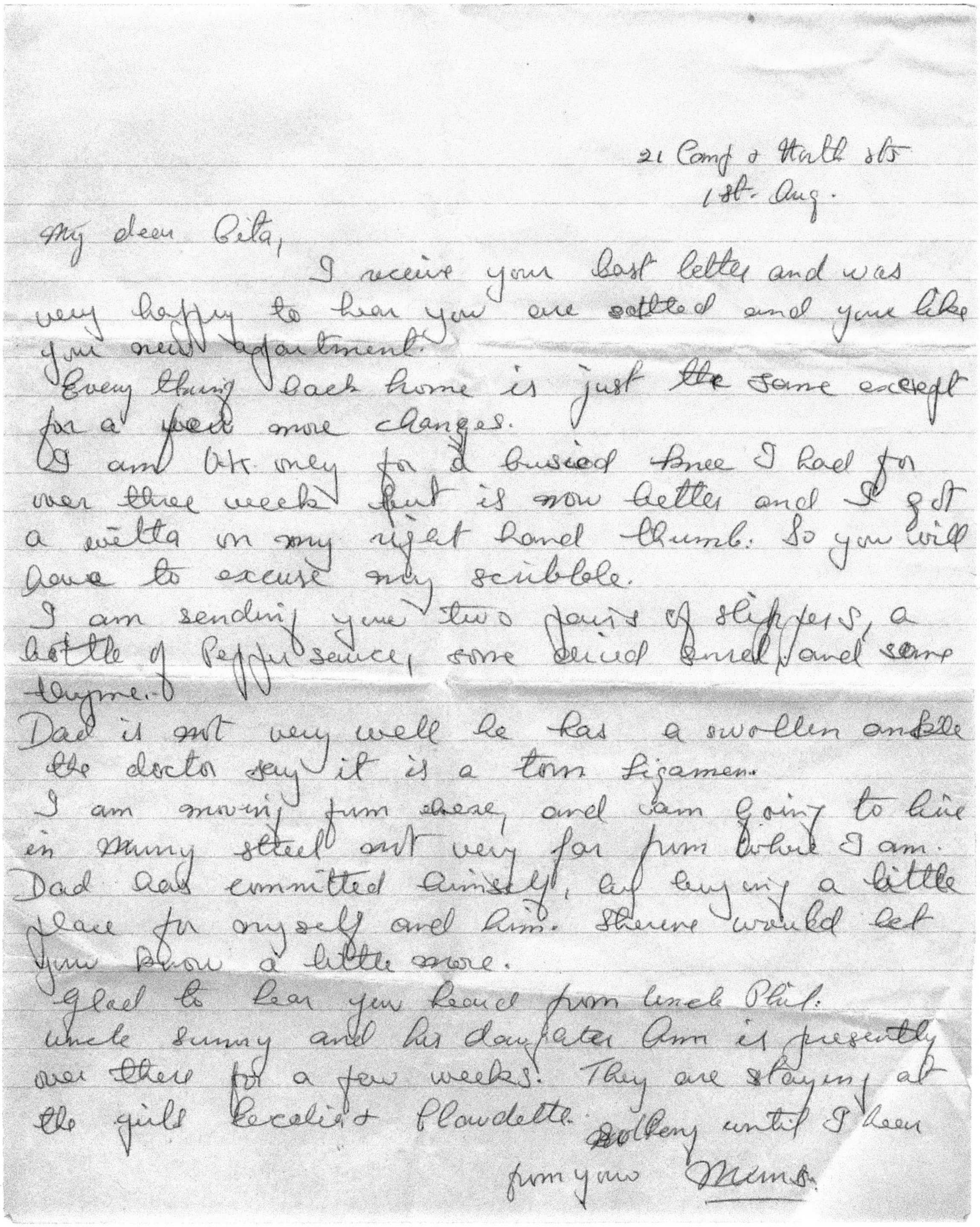

21 Camp & Harth sts
18t. Aug.

My dear Rita,

I receive your last letter and was very happy to hear you are settled and you like your new apartment.

Every thing back home is just the same except for a few more changes.

I am btr only for a busied knee I had for over three week but is now better and I got a welta on my right hand thumb. So you will have to excuse my scribble.

I am sending you two pairs of slippers, a bottle of Pepper sauce, some dried bread, and some thyme.

Dad is not very well he has a swollen ankle the doctor say it is a torn ligamen.

I am moving fum here, and I am going to live in many street not very far fum where I am. Dad has committed himself, of buying a little place for myself and him. I never would let you know a little more.

Glad to hear you heard from uncle Phil. uncle sunny and his daughter Ann is presently over there for a few weeks. They are staying at the girl Cecelia & Claudette.

Bolkey until I hear from your Mam.

Figure 2.4

Undated letter from my grandmother to my mother, sent between 1973 to 1976.

On the Time Before Us

Erika: There was a time before us; a time when we were strangers.

Cita: There was?

Erika: Yes.

Cita: When was that?

Erika: A time that I could look back to in pictures and see me in you, but you couldn't see me back then like you see me now.

Cita: Ah, okay.

Erika: You didn't always know me, you know!

Cita: Yeah, okay.

[laughter]

This is how our discussion begins before I open the spiral bound, tan colored—almost deceivingly gold–photo album that sits precariously at the edge of the table where we sit.

There she is (not as she sits before me). Newspapers strewn on a table in the background and on the floor at the base of the wooden rocking chair she leans back in (Fig. 2.5). Those lines have also been read, but by her? Are her fingertips blackened with ink? There she sits with the book open hovering above her lap between pinching thumbs and closed fingers. I imagine she is ever so gently balancing on the tips of her toes. Geometric shapes mirror the windowpanes making patterns on her hand-sewn skirt, the hem of which, when seated, meets the edge of the chair. Perhaps in red, orange, yellow, and green threads? She corrects me. In mustard yellow and beige. Legs long. Her hair neatly pinned up with a handful of black bobby pins. There she was. In a room of windows. There is a solitude. I could ask and should ask and must ask questions and I do, and she answers, but these aren't the questions nor the answers I want to ask and know. I want to know about all that is left out of the frame. I want to know which word her eyes rested on when this moment was seized and what imagery sat behind those eyes.

She looks up from her book. I have never seen her before. Never before with a smile somewhat unburdened. Who stole this moment from her? Her left hand, fingers spread on her lap.

There is a comfort in all this looking back at what was and will never be again except for in the faint remnants; the residue that stains. This comfort. It's deceiving. I can look back and speculate. I can look back. But there is a depth. One too entrenched in the *then* I am not privy to. Only so much. Over there in that photograph where I have never been and cannot gain entrance.

When she is looking off to the side with hands clasped below her right knee, it is then. This expression is one that I recognize. She has gone inside herself. She is looking at nothing and something and everything. The nylon webbing on the folding chair leaving imprints on the tanned skin of her thighs. I once thought that there was a time when she was most present to herself. This was what I thought of the time before us; the time when we were strangers.

Erika: Were you happy then?

Cita: Looking back at it, I don't think I was totally happy. I always felt like something was missing.

Figure 2.5

Cita at a bed and breakfast in New Amsterdam, Guyana, ca. 1965.

On Pre-Mourning

It is what composes the essence of being. Having done it on many occasions, I should have a greater understanding of the differences between being and having been, and the never going to be of human being human. It is not an understanding of it all that I have, but an awareness of its insistence. The way it sits and rests and threads itself. The way it kneads and punctures and erupts. Deep within this cavity. Derrida has whispered to me. First about the politics of friendships and then about this. He has said to me that in all friendships one will be left to mourn the other. We know this yet we keep it as murmurs in hushed tones and low voices until there is a fissure and it becomes.

I don't have to close my eyes to recall this. This that exasperated my fear of the void that loss carves. The rain was sudden. Everything was tinny and heavy and dank. My chest tightened. I could see it. I could see the rain falling with little to no space between each drop and the street flooding. My mother levitated higher and higher. On her back. Arms and legs choreographed gracefully flailing as the water quickly, yet simply, swept her away. This time I was certain that it could be this rain that would take her away from me.

What I wrestle with is the preparation. The anticipation of the unpredictability and its permanence. All before it happens. Before it happens without repetition.

It is our names that will survive us.

On Death

The photograph is an odd size, rectangular in shape with curved edges, aged. The face of it is faded and all colors look to be muted, bleached. She lays there still, unmoved. When we see people laying with their eyes unflinching like that with their hands folded like that, we know. Call it to mind. The last time my mother returned, she returned to cicadas' warning from trees, to that natural dampness of flesh, to bananas that are as sweet as they are yellow, to pulpy genips picked, to tamarind trees, jack fruits, sapodillas, paw paws, and mirrors covered when lightning strikes. The last time my mother returned, I read in the letters on lines that remain straight that she, my grandmother, wasn't feeling well, wasn't feeling right, wasn't feeling like herself. That last time she returned she believed that her presence wasn't known. I question that. An unarticulated distance emerged in a shared space where breaths were taken, held, and exhumed from the body. It, the body, becomes slightly smaller, lungs no longer stretching. With slender fingers she fixed her mother's hair while she lay there unmoved, still.

It pervades. It conjures itself without permission. It incites fear and held tongues. When I look at that photograph, I see my grandmother as my mother as myself. There is a truth. Each one before is a rehearsal for the next. And so, I must prepare. And so, I must work towards making the impermanent permanent, with death masks made from icing and tears caught in lachrymatory bottles and stitches recording time. The crux of it all are those moments spent together making all previous efforts futile. Or so one would think. It produces an unyielding echo.

On Memory

The photographs behind plastic sleeves serve as traces. She remembers being no older than six years old. Hand washing her brother's socks in buckets and sweeping wooden floors. Dragging her tiny finger along the insides of big, off-white enamel bowls lined with white icing. Inscribed measurements of raisins and prunes soaking in a large earthenware cork topped jar, which now sits in the corner of our kitchen. It, too, is a trace. The sweet smell of rum. Egg whites, icing sugar, almond essence, freshly squeezed lime juice. My grandmother, her mother, made and decorated cakes as a way of earning money. She taught classes in her small house around a table to women who would bring their own cakes and learn how to make roses with icing atop sweet drink bottle caps (Fig. 2.6 and Fig. 2.7). Pink. Blue. Green leaves were always green. Yellow. Orange. To prepare. To keep. To keep alive. To maintain. To make lasting. To preserve. To make this, us, me and she, tangible and permanent. Absurd growths of flowers and leaves arranged on our faces in purple and yellow. Hardened powdered icing sugar. These masks as sculptural objects—substitutions for the real—embed a timelessness in the moment after one's death. The unpleasant reminder of the persistence of impermanence. The flowers and leaves eroding, sliding, slowly down our faces from the heat that escaped our bodies.

And so, the repetition continues.

Figure 2.6

My grandmother teaches women in her neighborhood in Georgetown the art of baking and icing cakes, ca. late 1960s.

Figure 2.7

My grandmother in Georgetown poses with a wedding cake she made and decorated, ca. late 1960s.

In this work, 'The Impossible Speech Act' (Fig 2.8 and Fig. 2.9), my mother Cita is both subject and collaborator. Drawing on the teachings of my grandmother Angela, my mother and I take turns to hand-fashion face masks out of green, yellow, and purple icing. The diptych featured here is the final two portraits of the process. These repeated actions situate my mother psychically closer to her homeland as she remembers it, but only places me further away.

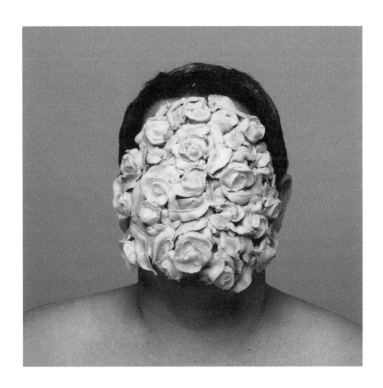

Figure 2.8 and Figure 2.9
Erika DeFreitas, 'The Impossible Speech Act' (detail)
2007, archival inkjet print.

On My Mother, My Mother's Mother, and I

It is in the way that the gathering of these letters cannot encapsulate each and every thing, yet I, we, continue to try for the sake of remembrance and the act of archiving. Commemoration. I think it is in the banter. It is in the way she will cook pepper pot, salt fish and bakes, beef curry with both chickpeas and potatoes, fried plantain, and black-eyed peas, just because she knows. It is in the way we silently exchange glances with eyebrows that gradually rise. The way she still braids my wet hair, strands clinging to her fingers. The way we dispute to repute what may have been hinted at with said eyebrows. It is in the laughter that ensues. It is in the listening, the participating, the engaging. The way the veins in our hands mirror the other. It is in our hands. It is in the way our voices merge and become indecipherable to those on the other end. The way she says in jest you (I) will miss me (her) when I'm (she's) gone.

Her and I and those who came before and will come after us continue to develop this matrilineal consciousness consisting of singularities and multiplicities that have woven themselves, presented themselves. The past and present self (selves) contains the other (others). There is a matriarchal lineage that endures and rejects omission despite memories that may be pieced together with inaccuracies, illusive details, unintentional omissions. Collectively writing and rewriting unwritten narratives. They are ever present. They are in the darkness below my eyes, the bridge of my nose, the slight curve in the nape of my neck, the length of my fingers, the pain in my joints and in the crevices that are etched into, mapped onto my skin.

All that I have is tucked into my pockets. Some of it lingers in my clenched fists. Some of it is hushed in the pleats near my eyes. Kept between toes and under nails. Some of it is intertwined with strands of my hair conceiving tight curls. In the thick of. Under. In the alcove below my tongue and in the seams between my teeth. Yes. Most of it. Most of it nests itself in my bones. All biding time. All taking form.

Notes

1. Interview between Erika DeFreitas and Cita DeFreitas, Toronto, Canada, 12 June 2016.

3.

Electric Dreams

—

Natalie Hopkinson and Serena Hopkinson

Figure 3.1

Serena Hopkinson on a class trip to Trinidad in 1966 while she was a student at St. Joseph's High School in Georgetown, Guyana.

      https://doi.org/10.11647/OBP.0218.04

On the Move

Mom, these days when I see all the xenophobia and nastiness in the United States, I am overwhelmed by an urge to pick up and move. Growing up, you and dad were constantly on the go. I think I counted eighteen addresses in two countries and three states before I finished undergrad. That you and dad could both come from the humblest of Guyanese families, land in North America with no visa, and then sail into an upper middle-class life is pretty amazing. Our family's migrations speak to the choices we can all make as educated people with skills in demand, and as global citizens.

You and dad never settled. You never stopped moving, exploring, hoping, dreaming, and demanding something better for yourselves and for us. You never really got comfortable. You fell—a lot. But you never seemed to spend a lot of time on regrets. You were always on the lookout for a new, better thing.

Mom, I am so proud that you have gone back to undergrad at Florida Atlantic University to study sociology and Spanish. You are always talking about ways to improve your oral fluency. At sixty-eight! If you can be that courageous and mentally nimble as you approach sixty-nine, with all you have been through, it makes me feel that I, too, can face any challenge in front of me. When you walk across that stage to collect your undergraduate degree this year, no one will be cheering louder or longer than me.

Natalie

Bush People

Natalie, I have spent so much of my life building, and then starting over again. Moving is awful. It's a pain. But it is so thrilling. Each time, I feel reborn. I started out in the country on the Pomeroon River, moved to the city of Georgetown where I married your dad, left Guyana, became a Canadian citizen. I had you four kids in Canada and moved to the US. I had careers in banking, accounting, computer tech, and real estate. I rebuilt our family after divorce. I had to rebuild my body from cancer—twice. But when I consider where I draw my strength, who I am deep inside, I know I can face any difficult situation in life because, as I proudly say, 'I am from the Bush!'

My mother, Christina (Tina) Elizabeth Baird, was primarily Arawak and my dad, Millington Benn, was African. I am their second child of nine children. I was born in 1948, at home near the river with the help of a midwife. Until I left in 1960, we never had a motorboat, so we always paddled wherever we wanted to go. Each Monday, there was a passenger launch that picked up people on both banks of the Pomeroon to go to Charity—a big market where everyone took their goods to sell. Charity was also the connecting point to a road that took people to other places in Guyana. It was a special hub filled with laughter and friends.

The Pomeroon River was ominous at night. It was usually dark by 6 p.m. and bright with sunlight by 6 a.m. We were very close to the equator. We had no clock. We estimated the time by the position of the sun during the day. We looked on the steps of the house to see where the shadows were. When it rained and there was no sun in the sky we had to guess. I can still smell the river at night. It is a moldy, haunting, muddy, deathly smell. Pitch black. There were small kerosene bottle lamps around and often a big fire to send swarms of mosquitoes away.

At times when I used to smell the river, I would wonder which person it might have claimed that day. Seventy-five feet deep, the Pomeroon River had no mercy. It didn't matter how much of a great swimmer you were, when it was ready to take you, it did. One time, my brother Ovid had to rescue me when I panicked attempting to swim across it. As children, we paddled for two or three miles on the other side of the river to the Marlborough Roman Catholic School. How long the trip took depended on the tide—whether it was coming in or out, whether it was stormy or not, whether the waves were high or low. Some of our schoolmates did not make it. Their boats capsized and they drowned. That all nine of us survived our crossings of that river for so many years, still surprises me.

But the Pomeroon River also provided our transportation and sustained our lives. We drank the brown water. We bathed in it. We swam in it. We fished in it. It fed us: dried, curried, stewed, and fried fish for school almost every day. The mighty, mighty Pomeroon River was home until I was twelve.

Serena

Snow White

Mom, I remember my first time visiting the Pomeroon was the first time I saw you scared. In 1984 all of us—Michael, Denise, Nicole, and Dad—were all packed onto that tiny speedboat on the Essequibo River on our way to your childhood home. I was eight years old and all I had known was Edmonton, Canada. We got our hair braided in cornrows. Someone put a flower in my hair. I don't remember wearing any life jackets.

All that we saw and experienced in Guyana was so different from our lives in Canada. We got to taste what were mostly rare treats in Edmonton. We ate lots of cassava bread, plantain chips, pepper pot, garlic pork, and curry chicken. In Georgetown, city buses were packed with people moving and speaking fast. Rasta hairstyles, thick and matted, stretched down to people's waists. I learned to chew on a sugarcane stalk and saw it cut fresh with a cutlass. We learned where our family's accents came from. You and dad were so jubilant and at ease, enjoying a triumphant return 'back home.'

We arrived so pasty pale because we got little sun in Canada. For us kids, it was a strange new experience. But as I started to grow older and more aware of race, Canada was also beginning to feel a bit strange, too. In Edmonton, we were born into constant snow. We lived in our boots and ski pants and some of our time on the playground during recess was for skating. The Edmonton I remember was filled with ballet classes, badminton practice, tennis, gymnastics, the Royal Glenora country club, and lots of travel. It was a cold city filled with warm, friendly people. I can't say I feel the same connection to Edmonton as you do to the Pomeroon River. But, I, too, love the city of my birth and am grateful to be born there.

Natalie

Daddy's Girl

Natalie, to me my dad will always represent 'home.' He was very serious, quiet, and hardworking. I adored him. He was what Guyanese call the ultimate 'sweetman.' He loved the ladies. But he was also a thirty-something-year-old married man when my mixed-race and Amerindian mother, at sixteen years old, became pregnant with my older sister Lynette. My mom grew up in an environment where it was normal to violate young indigenous girls. My dad had two children from his marriage and numerous others outside his marriage. At last count, the number was twenty-two children with multiple women. When he died in 1988 at age seventy-four, he had a four-year-old son with another indigenous woman. When we lived in the Pomeroon, my siblings never wanted to talk to him. They were intimidated. I was not.

In 1960, when I was almost twelve, the teachers of the Marlborough Roman Catholic School told my parents to send me to take an exam far away. Details were scarce. My dad arranged it. Afterward, we learned that students who passed it were allowed to go to secondary school in the capital, Georgetown. And so, my journey away from the Pomeroon River began. Dad decided he would do whatever was necessary to keep me in school. He became the most important person in my life. I bade farewell to my river home and went to St. Joseph's High School in Georgetown, a Catholic girl's convent school with 600 girls. It was a brand-new beautiful school located in a very prime and fancy stretch of real estate. Everyone wore blue and white uniforms. I was totally out of place. I was not accustomed to wearing shoes. My feet hurt and I was uncomfortable every single day. My fellow schoolmates were children of wealthy parents—business people, diplomats, and educated expats.

My end-of-school term trips home from Georgetown took me twelve hours: a bus to Stabroek Market, a ferry to Vreedenhoop, a train to Parika, a steamer to Adventure, a bus on an unpaved road for forty miles to Charity, and finally a passenger launch to Grant Strong Hope on the bank of the Pomeroon River. There were no roads.

Going to St. Joseph's pushed me into another world. Dad was always proud to introduce me to people who didn't know me as 'my daughter who is away at school.' I was a celebrity. It was dad who agreed to send me on a field trip to Trinidad with my rich schoolmates in 1965. At home mom, dad, and my eight siblings farmed coconuts, oranges, limes, cucumbers, rice, and corn on about five acres of land. To pay for the trip, my siblings had to harvest more produce to sell at the market. Back then, I felt entitled to the trip. Now, I cringe at my lack of self-awareness, and how I must have seemed to my siblings. They had to sacrifice to give me an opportunity they never got.

British Guiana had always been a country with conflicts over race. It mattered whether one was African, Indian, or Portuguese. Your race determined your status. I am one of those mixed-up ones—split between my mom's mixed Amerindian heritage and my father's African ancestry. In the Caribbean caste system, African ranks higher than indigenous Amerindian, who were often exploited. My mom, my siblings and I were never really accepted. We were referred to as 'buck children.'

Serena

Figure 3.2

Serena Hopkinson (far left) in 1967 with her fellow students at St. Joseph's High School, Georgetown, Guyana.

Daddy's Girl, Part II

Mom, we have this in common: we both spent the first decade of our lives in our birthplace before we made our first migration—when everything changed abruptly. For you, it was leaving 'Bush life' on the Pomeroon River for the big city Georgetown. For me, it was leaving Edmonton, Canada for a whole other country—Indiana, United States.

Growing up in Edmonton, most of my playmates were white Canadians, but a good number of the kids were also the children of immigrants from different countries—China, Pakistan, Thailand, Yugoslavia, Czechoslovakia, Ukraine, and Italy. I remember one solitary Jamaican but no other Blacks in our school.

Canadian manners dictated that it was rude to mention race. I started having questions as I approached puberty. In *Études Sociales* class, we talked about the 'White Man' who conquered and oppressed the First Nation indigenous Canadians. I wondered, 'Where did I fit?' Didn't our family come here to inhabit their land, too? We must be considered the 'White Man!' I was happy at this thought. At a sleepover, the girls went around a circle confessing their crushes. When eyes stopped at me, I shyly spit out the name of a white boy in our class. Everyone smiled politely, and then a silence hung two beats too long. Weeks later, I daydreamed. Who *would* I marry? For the first time, I felt my difference. It was a bit lonely.

It helped to be part of our large family. The four of us were like a gang. Michael and Nicole—so smart, athletic, artistically talented, and popular—blazed the path for me and Denise. But in 1986, in fourth grade, dad took the job in Indiana installing a new computer system for the Department of Motor Vehicles. Everything changed for our gang of six. I watched you cry as dad flew back and forth weekly from Edmonton and Indianapolis. Dad's absences also hit me hard. I often could not hold back my tears in school. I, too, was a 'Daddy's girl.' Of the four of us kids, I looked the most like him. I loved to snuggle underneath him. I was always sad when he commuted to his job in Indiana and cried at school sometimes. A school counselor put together a calendar to count the days when he would be coming back home. Like anyone else, he had his flaws. He could occasionally be cruel. Things only got worse when we moved to Indiana.

Natalie

'Black Bitch'

In 1963, when I was fifteen years old, tensions over race and politics boiled over. In Georgetown where I went to school, there were fierce riots and violence between Africans and Indians who were vying for political power as we approached independence from Great Britain. The whole of downtown Georgetown was burnt to smithereens. I had to miss school for months while things simmered down. Because I looked ambiguous—I was brown-skinned but wore my soft curls blown straight—I didn't know whether I would be attacked in the streets by Indians or Africans.

I had a major crush on an Indian boy—Bishnue. He was forbidden by his parents from speaking to me. We found a way though. His family had chosen an Indian girl for him. She lived not far from me in a large fancy Georgetown home. One day, she called me a 'Black bitch.' I attacked her and threw her off her bicycle. She was hurt. Her dad was a sheriff. He went to my very prestigious school and demanded I be kicked out. I was so scared. I don't really know how I was spared.

Serena

'Martian'

Beech Grove, Indiana in the 1980s was a strange and intense place. Everyone spoke with a twang, a slow and lazy tongue. Everywhere we went in the neighborhood, hateful stares demanded answers I did not have. I sensed the Hopkinson family had caused the people of Beech Grove a great offense. No one told me what. We spoke English, so people expected us to know and understand things. We did not. Like: if you are the only Black family, there is probably a reason for that. Each time I opened my mouth, it was so obvious how different I was from white kids who were our neighbors in Beech Grove. I was a Martian to the Black kids bused in by desegregation court order from inner city Indianapolis. Instead of speaking in the wrong accent and being outed for not knowing the slang or music, I chose silence. Michael and I had a job delivering newspapers as we did in Canada. We had to go door-to-door to collect our payment. I could never predict what level of disgust flung open on the other side of the door. I remember when teenagers chased Michael as he walked home, screaming at him, '*KKK is gonna get you, nigger!*'

Compared to the bright whiteness and cheer of Canada, Indiana was heavy and dark. I tried to make myself small. I strained to avoid drawing attention to myself. I wanted to stay off the streets. But home ceased to be a refuge as we turned our frustration and anger inward in our too-tiny apartment. We wanted to rent or buy a bigger house in Beech Grove, but every single white seller or renter refused our family. You and dad fought constantly. My daily wish was to turn invisible and thus never anger anyone inside or outside our house. I dreamed of running and floating far away.

Natalie

Torn Asunder

Natalie, those were hard times in Beech Grove. I can relate to the alienation you felt. I don't know how I held on to my sanity. My marriage did not survive. Living without friends and family in Indiana, I turned inward for peace. As my marriage crumbled, I continued running and playing tennis every day. In these activities, I challenged myself physically. I entered my first half-marathon, training weekly with my new white friends in this suburb. We had absolutely no Black neighbors. When our constant and increasingly vicious fights became too much to bear, I calmly called a sharp young attorney from the yellow pages. He advised me that in Indiana, no woman should take it for granted that she will get custody of the children.

I proceeded anyhow with the divorce, praying feverishly that I could convince the judge that I could care for four children even though I was not working at the time. What optimism! My huge character flaw—but it often worked. The judge gave me full custody. I am so sorry for the pain these years caused you.

Serena

Finding Home

Mom, I don't like it when you blame yourself. Beech Grove was an outlier. In general, people have treated me well. You and dad divorced, and we moved to Indianapolis into an excellent and racially mixed school district. I can't say that the white kids on the north side welcomed me with open arms, but they were not hostile. And to this day my oldest and dearest friends are Black friends I made in Indianapolis. School was always a refuge for me. It was a place that was orderly, not messy. So, I am grateful to you for making sure we lived in the very best school districts available, even if at times we did not live in the grandest house.

In the years you worked as the business manager at the historic Black Madame C.J. Walker Theatre in Indianapolis, I started to come out of the shell I had erected around myself. While dad was focused on Michael becoming the next tennis superstar, you signed us girls up for all of the theatre's 'Youth in Arts' programs. We did dance, drama, creative writing, and visual art. And for the first time in my life, I was around a lot of other Black people. It felt like I was able to exhale after holding my breath for years without realizing it.

When I got the opportunity to go to Howard University in Washington, DC on a journalism scholarship, I was happy to continue my journey of exploring identity, understanding my place in the world, and finding out 'what is home.' I met my future husband Rudy McGann there. I stayed and built my family. I have now lived in

Washington, DC longer than I have lived anywhere else. It has been the closest thing to 'home' for me. In 2008, I voted for the first time, for Barack Obama. Those eight years in America and in Washington, DC have been a fairy tale. With that beautiful Obama family in The White House, I allowed myself to fully exhale: to believe that yes, this was my country; I belonged here; this *was* home. For now.

Natalie

Finding Love

Natalie, I am so proud of what you have done as an academic. It is maybe what I would have done if I were born at a different time, when the options and expectations for women were different.

In 1965, I managed to finish high school at the top of my class and St. Joseph's offered to extend my scholarship to do advanced level subjects for the next two years. By 1967, I had graduated from St. Joseph's High School and found my first job at a Georgetown accounting firm as an audit clerk. A year later, I moved on to Barclays Bank. At that time the banks only hired Portuguese or 'high-colored' people—meaning light-skinned. With my curly hair and my rich brown skin, I became the first Black teller there.

Around that time, I met your dad. Terrence Hopkinson graduated from the top high school for boys, Queen's College. He was tall and good-looking with a mischievous dimple in his chin. It was 1969 and he was just back from traveling overseas, working for IBM in Trinidad and Barbados and in Texas and New York. He was the best player on the badminton courts. I was one of three girls who played, and I was an in-your-face kind of player. We played as doubles partners until we won the national mixed-doubles championship the next year and represented Guyana in tournaments abroad. We did not have a winning record, but we did win at our relationship. We got married in 1970. Terrence wanted to go to Canada to continue school. He made a lot of connections working for IBM maintaining computers throughout the Caribbean and training in the US. But he knew he could not advance any further at IBM if he did not get his college degree. He did not like what he was hearing about the draft to fight in Vietnam in the US, so we chose to move to Canada.

I had no money. He had some. Neither of our families had money to help. I approached my bank manager and asked to borrow $3,600. I had no collateral, but I assured him that I'd pay it back. He wrote me the check on my word. We left Guyana in 1970 and paid back the loan four years later.

After our airfare and other expenses, Terry and I landed in Toronto with $103. Immigration asked us how long we wanted to stay. We said we would be going to the

Figure 3.3

Serena and Terrence Hopkinson on their wedding day in 1970 in Georgetown, Guyana.

Figure 3.4

Serena and Terrence Hopkinson in their first year in Toronto, Canada, 1970.

University of Toronto. They gave us ninety days to get our student visas. We went to the University, found out about the high fees and realized that going to university was not going to happen that year. Instead, we petitioned the Canadian government for 'landed immigrant status' to allow us to stay and work.

Between your dad and me, we had no doubt that all of it was going to turn out as we planned. He had the ideas and the suggestions, and I worked on making them happen. Immigration officers asked whether we had any family or friends out west. We said yes and we used our last dollars for airfare to Edmonton. We got our Canadian resident status within three months. I eventually got a job with the Alberta government. Your dad finished his bachelor's degree in computer science at the University of Alberta, then went on to do his MBA while working at major companies and owning his own business. During those years we also sponsored my mother and three brothers to join us in Edmonton. I worked to support your dad's studies, went to college in the summers, and raised you four children. We became popular for our parties and hangouts for our club friends, college friends, and Caribbean friends. We acted in plays as a family. It was a good life in Edmonton.

Serena

A Return to Guyana

Mom, you were with me in 2010, at Mrs. Hing's funeral in New York at the moment my interest in Guyana was rekindled. I hadn't been back since that childhood trip. I was so intrigued by the conversation we had with Uncle Ovid after the funeral at a restaurant in the Little Guyana part of Queens. Of course, we talked about Mrs. Hing, the beautiful Chinese-Guyanese matriarch whose home you boarded at during your studies at St. Josephs and who taught us all how to make fried rice and stir-fry. Uncle Ovid was missing Guyana bad. He reminisced about his old life and adventures he had hunting gold and diamonds as an underwater miner. I loved his stories of diving underwater for hours and camping in the forest with makeshift gold-mining villages deep in the interior hinterlands. It brought back memories of my first visit to the Pomeroon. Uncle Ovid was one of the last siblings to migrate to North America and he was already in his fifties. He was living in New York and working as a security guard. He complained that he was 'gettin' fat' due to this new sedentary lifestyle, and not enjoying America at all. He told me he was biding his time until he could go 'back home.' This was very odd to me. To hear most Guyanese, the only direction there was supposed to be in Guyana was 'out.' You and dad sent for everyone who wanted to make the crossing. Dad never had any desire to return. He always used to say he had no friends in Guyana because everyone left. 'Brain drain,' he called it.

Uncle Ovid's melancholy surprised and intrigued me. I was determined to go to Guyana and learn more about this place that so tugged at him. I wanted to see the beauty and adventure he could not wait to get back to when he retired.

I was very happy to be able to plan a month-long trip in 2011 with four generations of our family in Guyana. Gramma Tina (who came to Canada in 1979), you, Rudy, and the kids joined us. Our kids Maverick and Maven, eleven and eight years old at the time, were able to participate in a children's heritage camp sponsored by the Guyana National Trust. We stayed in Uncle Richard Hing's apartment, which had no TV or air conditioning. We visited the gold mines and stayed in a country home like the one you lived in on the Pomeroon River. I made some local research contacts for a project I was working on art and public policy.

In the last six years, I have since returned to Guyana on my own and reconnected on Facebook and in person with my first cousins who still live there. I got a publishing contract for a book about artists set in Guyana. In my readings, travels, and interviews, I've learned so much about our idiosyncratic ways. So much is explained by tracing Guyana's jagged path of colonization and globalization, like why we have five continents represented in our food and culture. I learned so much about these historic, economic, and cultural clashes that shaped who we are. I'm happy to be able to pass these experiences on to my children and their children, and for posterity through my writing about Guyana. It is wonderful to hear about how you, too, have returned.

Natalie

Electric Dreams

On 12 May 2016 I arrived in Guyana for the 50th Anniversary of Independence celebrations. The pomp and ceremonies were fine, but I was very antsy about leaving to go 'down to the Pomeroon' as we say. My boyfriend (also named Rudy) took the trip with me. We took a crowded minibus downtown and then another one that took us to Parika where we hopped into a speedboat with forty other passengers. Today we have life jackets; it is now a law to provide them. Traveling close to the mouth of the Essequibo River, which at its widest is nineteen miles, the trip took us about forty-five minutes. The river was choppy. The waves slapped the bottom of the boat. I thought, *this frigging boat is going to disintegrate at any time*. I breathed deeply and calmed down, remembering these waters were familiar to me since birth.

We sped by the islands of Leguan and Wakenaam. For a brief moment we could see no shoreline. We were at the mouth of the Essequibo River as it flowed into the Atlantic Ocean. We arrived at Supenaam, and my brother sent transportation for me. By car we traveled forty miles to Charity on a single road. Both sides were filled with rice fields, coconut fields, and stores. There were very large beautiful homes situated on many acres of land. It was dreamy. It would be so lovely to live in this area again.

At the end of this road was Charity. The market was busier than I recalled. We got into my cousin Roy's speedboat, fueled up, and drove towards Marlborough Roman Catholic School, my old primary school. I got out of the speedboat and walked toward one of the buildings. There was no guard there. I approached the headmistress. When she told me there was no power in the school that was serving over a hundred beautiful children, most of them indigenous, I was appalled. There was no electrical power when I left nearly sixty years ago. And there was no electrical power now. No electricity means no plumbing, no stoves, no computers, no phones, no printers, no copiers, no Internet. There are still no paved roads. The closest hospital is about six miles away and you can only get there by speedboat or canoe.

When I returned to the city, I realized that in part the reason Marlborough was forgotten was because they are out of sight, out of mind. I visited my nephew Carlos, a civil engineering student at the University of Guyana, and we talked about solar energy. Together, we met with the Departments of Education and Public Works. They accepted my offer to underwrite the cost of wiring the Marlborough school buildings. Carlos became my project manager. We hired an electrician to wire the main building. The Department of Education delivered donated solar panels and two computers. The work continues to move forward via email, Facebook, Western Union, and telephone. The next step is to train the staff and students on how to use their new technology.

I hope they keep celebrating the 'Bush' culture that makes us special, too.

Between my busy tennis schedule, finishing coursework for my bachelor's degree in sociology and Spanish, and bringing electricity to my elementary school in Guyana, I have been thinking about what is next. I have dreams of spending a year in Barcelona to improve my Spanish fluency. I hope you and the family will come and visit me there, too.

Serena

PART II
THE ONES WHO LEAVE . . .
THE ONES WHO ARE LEFT

We were a straggly bunch of immigrants
in a lily white landscape.
We made our home among strangers,
knowing no one but ourselves.

Meiling Jin, 'Strangers in A Hostile Landscape'[1]

There are two spectrums of the migration arc: *the ones who leave and the ones who are left*. The act of migration is an act of reciprocity—to leave a place we reconcile that we must leave others behind. Yet, the narratives of the ones who are left are constantly eclipsed. Part II, *The Ones Who Leave . . . the Ones Who Are Left*, counters the discourse and creative representations on migration that are overwhelmingly focused on the ones who leave. Contributors Dominique Hunter (Guyana), Khadija Benn (Guyana), Ingrid Griffith (United States), and I, Grace Aneiza Ali (United States), center the stories of those who remain.

In 'The Geography of Separation,' I, **Grace Aneiza Ali** write about women and girls who have known both spectrums of the migration arc: to leave and to be left. The essay is a travelogue, composed of four vignettes, each focusing on a woman or girl I've encountered in a precise moment in time and in a particular place—Guyana, India, and Ethiopia. Each abstract is framed as an 'Arrival' or 'Departure' to situate my accountability to these places and to the ways I've entered into or departed the lives of the people who live there. Twenty-five years after my first departure from Guyana and many miles circling the globe since, all roads still seem to lead back to Guyana. Whether I am in Hyderabad or Harrar or Harlem, I find myself weaving the stories of these places and the people I've encountered with those of Guyana. For now, this is how I psychically return. And yet I know it is not enough. In her collection of memoir-essays, *Create Dangerously: The Immigrant Artist at Work*, the Haitian-American writer Edwidge Danticat examines what it means to write stories about a land she no longer lives in. 'Some of us think we are accidents of literacy,' she says.[2] Each time I board a plane for another far-off land, I grapple with the guilt that it is not bound for Guyana. I am haunted by the what-ifs. What if I had stayed? What kind of stories should I be telling of Guyana? What do I owe this country? Am I guilty, too, of forgetting?

 https://doi.org/10.11647/OBP.0218.05

Guyanese-born artist **Dominique Hunter**, based in the nation's capital city of Georgetown, moves in and out of several geographic spaces within the Caribbean and North America for various artist residencies and opportunities. They are what she calls 'mini migrations.' Yet, she is vocal about rooting her artistic practice in Guyana, even while it is subjected to the ebb and flow of departure. In her art essay, 'Transplantation,' Hunter tells us that from a very young age, the Guyanese citizen is indoctrinated with the charge to leave their country. 'There is an expectation once you have reached a certain age: pack what you can and leave. I am well past that age, yet I remain, stubbornly rooted in the land my parents spent their lives cultivating,' she writes. What a spectacular thing for any citizen of any place to grapple with—to be, from birth, dispossessed of one's own land. As both artist and citizen in Guyana, we are shown how she shoulders the personal, political, and economic consequences of Guyanese leaving their native land in droves. In her essay, Hunter uses a dictionary definition of 'transplantation' as a metaphorical device to engage ideas of migration and rootedness. She shepherds us through what she deems, 'A guide to surviving transplantation and other traumas.' In both her words and collages, Hunter layers organic imagery reminiscent of Guyana's lush vegetation found in its interior Amazon as well as on its riverbeds and the famous Sea Wall on the coast of the Atlantic Ocean. Embedded in her visual imagery is a silhouetted self-referential figure. Its haunting presence among the flora and fauna thrives amidst Guyana's extreme elements of temperature, wind, water, and sand. In this symbolic artistic gesture, Hunter insists that the act of staying, of being rooted, of choosing not to be transplanted, is its own kind of agency.

Like Hunter, **Khadija Benn** is among the few women photographers living in Guyana and choosing to forge an artistic practice. As a geospatial analyst, Benn often journeys across Guyana to remote places where most Guyanese rarely have access. These small villages are central to Benn's stunning black and white portraits of the elder Amerindian women who call these communities home. However, as she emphatically notes in her portraiture essay, 'Those Who Remain,' these are not invisible women. Benn's adjoining excerpts from her interviews with the Amerindian elders illustrate how essential they are to Guyana's history and its migration stories. These women, whose dates of birth begin as early as the 1930s, have witnessed Guyana evolve from a colonized British territory, to an independent state, to a nation struggling to carve out its identity on the world stage, to a country now burdened by its citizens departing. They have also been the ones most impacted by serious economic downturns over the past decade where the decline of mining industries, coupled with very little access to education beyond primary school, have left these communities with few or no choices to thrive. These elder Amerindian women are mothers, grandmothers, and great-grandmothers whose descendants have migrated to border countries like Venezuela and Brazil in South America, to North America, and to nearby Caribbean islands. Yet, these women have made the choice to stay. While their children go back and forth between Guyana and their newfound lands, many of these elders have never left Guyana, some have never left the villages they were born in, and some have no desire to leave.

At the age of seven, **Ingrid Griffith**'s parents left Guyana for the United States, leaving their children in the care of their grandmothers. Griffith's experience is common for many Guyanese as well as Caribbean families where parents must make the difficult choice to migrate and leave their children with extended family members or caregivers. It is indeed a noble agenda, as Griffith writes about her parents' goals to work hard in a foreign land so that they can acquire the funds, passports, and visas to have their children join them later in the United States—a process that took years. Told uniquely through Griffith's perspective as a young girl, 'When They Left' offers a glimpse of how a child struggles to reconcile her parents' love with their simultaneous departure. In her moving memoir essay, Griffith explores the rupture migration enacts on families when children are split apart from their parents and how that separation reverberates years after the first moment of departure. It is the narrative we rarely see—what the act of leaving means for a child and how it becomes an open wound of abandonment.

Collectively, the essays in *The Ones Who Leave . . . the Ones Who Are Left* underscore that with both ancestors and descendants long gone, the women and girls who remain in Guyana bear witness to the personal damage and the larger political consequences when a citizenry leaves its country. As migration swirls around them, Hunter, Griffith, Benn, and I, acknowledge leaving and being left as the great tension that twists all of our lives.

Notes

1. Epigraph from 'Strangers in A Hostile Landscape,' in *Gifts from My Grandmother* (London: Sheba Feminist Press, 1985), p. 20.

2. Edwidge Danticat, *Create Dangerously: The Immigrant Artist at Work* (New York: Vintage Books, 2011), p. 19.

4.

The Geography of Separation

—

Grace Aneiza Ali

Figure 4.1

Grace Aneiza Ali at the Sea Wall, Georgetown, Guyana, 2014, digital photography. Photo by Candace Ali-Lindsay.

 https://doi.org/10.11647/OBP.0218.06

DEPARTURE
8 April 1995
Georgetown, Guyana

The Things We Carry

On the eve of our 6:30 a.m. one-way flight bound for John F. Kennedy Airport, New York City, my mother called us into her bedroom for a family prayer. My little sister was only six years old at the time so she would remember nothing of the weightiness of that night. Because we were older, fourteen and fifteen, my brother and I understood the urgency of the moment. We sat on the bed, holding each other's hands with our eyes closed—like we always did in this ritual—as my mother prayed. It would be our last family prayer in Guyana. When she was done praying for our safety on the journey, she told us, 'When we get to America, nothing changes. We will still be who we are.'

By 10 p.m. our house had been gleaned of its remaining furniture, knick-knacks, linens, and kitchen wares—all the things we could not carry. The state of my mother's bedroom—ground zero for where our family had been packing five large suitcases for the past month—was relatively calm, considering this was the eve of our departure from our homeland. My mother was thankful that it wasn't one of the scheduled blackout nights in our part of Georgetown. At least there was electricity as she finished packing. The suitcases were zipped up and padlocked, except for hers. The jars of wiri wiri pepper sauce and mango achar, sealed in their thick masking tape, had already been weaved into the nooks between her clothing. My mom had one major problem left to solve. The large cast-iron karahi bulged under the layers of clothes she had carefully swaddled it in. There was no minimizing its presence in the suitcase. She knew with it the luggage would be over the weight limit. She also knew that to take the pot, she had to leave something behind.

A staple in every Guyanese kitchen, the karahi is a thick, circular, and deep cooking pot that originated in the Indian subcontinent. It was first introduced in Guyana by the Indian indentured servants who were brought by the British, beginning in 1838 and throughout the early 1900s, to work the sugar plantations and rice farms in then British Guiana. Our karahi—aged, scratched, chipped, nicked, scraped, and blackened—had hit its sweet spot. Over decades, it had absorbed into its pores the perfect medley of oils and spices, which it now infused into whatever meats, vegetables, and sauces were poured into it. My mother had grown up as a young girl watching her mother cook for her family in the same karahi. Daily, it produced curries or stews or an occasional chow mein or fried rice for my mother and her siblings. In her suitcase bound for America, there was no prized jewelry, no priceless antiques, no precious silk saris.

There was only the karahi—the sole possession she had after her mother died. It was not going to be left behind. It was coming to America with us.

On 8 April 1995, my mother departed Guyana and took her entire family with her. A singular document transformed my family from citizens in one land to aliens in another. Yet, it had taken ten years for our visas to be approved. My mother had spent a decade of her life in limbo between present and future, between living in one land and making plans for an uncertain one. As she prepared for that early April morning flight, a decade of waiting, of not knowing when we would leave, had come to an end.

At thirty-nine years old, my mother started over in a foreign land. She was leaving a homeland where the tragedies often eclipsed the joys. She was leaving a country she saw violently transition from a colonized territory to an independent republic. She was leaving a place where her father, haunted by the demons of alcoholism, took his life, adding to the statistics of Guyana's high suicide rates among Indian men. She was leaving a country where, just a few years after her father's death, her mother too would pass away at the young age of forty-eight after an aneurism gripped her brain. With her father's suicide and her mother's death, my mother was orphaned by nineteen years old. She was leaving a country on whose soil she buried her mother while still in mourning for her father. It was then her fear began: she too would not live past the age of fifty, as none of her parents did. The loss of her mother and father ushered in a series of constant departures. Beginning in the 1970s, her six siblings joined the exodus of Guyanese leaving Guyana. They moved on to Barbados, Canada, and the United States, without her.

My mother was leaving a country where, despite the constant companions of death and departure, she forged a family of her own. She was leaving a country that had seen her evolve from an orphaned daughter, to a wife, to a young mother. She was leaving a country where, like her mother and father, she too struggled to keep her children from the deep abyss of poverty. She was leaving a country where she had no infant formula for her babies because the government had banned foreign imports. 'Let them eat cornmeal,' they said. It was then that she began to understand the demons that plagued her father were not only of his own making. The failure to take care of his family ate away at him too. She was leaving Guyana with no desire to return.

Despite all of these things, or perhaps because of them, it was non-negotiable for my mother that the karahi come with us to America. It carried within its pores her memories of her mother. Twenty-five years later, it is the object that bridges my mother's past with her present, her homeland with her new land. After all these years, it survives. It is now over sixty years old. Oceans and lands apart from its origin, the karahi continues to nourish my family. My mother still cooks her curries and stews in that karahi in her American home. She is among the many daughters who carry our mother's things across borders.

ARRIVAL
24 September 2003
Hyderabad, Andra Pradesh, India

Indra

Indra sat cross-legged on the linoleum floor with her plate and cup centered neatly between her knees. She didn't have a spoon or fork. She ate with her hands. No kind of pleading, begging, hand gesturing, or angry faces I made to show my disapproval, would get her to move from the floor to the chair to eat at the table with me. Often, in an act of resistance to her act of defiance, I would take my plate and cup and sit on the floor with her. I would eat the rice and dahl with my hands, too. She would first laugh, then yell at me in Telugu, 'Pāgala!'

This was her way of cussing at me affectionately, calling me 'the crazy girl.' Indra didn't speak my English and I didn't speak her Telugu, the regional language of the state of Andhra Pradesh. We managed to meet in the middle in Hindi, the national language of India, because of our mutual attraction to Bollywood films. Indra was addicted to the love stories and the ballads. I used them as a Hindi language immersion course. Or so I pretended. Indra knew I was just as enthralled by the plots of forbidden love that always led to predictable happy endings. Life, and love for that matter, as depicted by Bollywood, was blissfully simple.

Indra spoke more languages than I did. In fact, while she spoke three Indian tongues—Telugu, Urdu, Hindi—my Telugu was non-existent, and my Hindi was severely limited. I couldn't utter a complete sentence or express a full thought in Hindi. What I knew were single words and could string together elementary phrases to offer to the city's rickshaw drivers to get me from point A to B on the Hyderabad streets. When I first arrived in Hyderabad, I tried taking Hindi lessons. The school taught Hindi by way of Telugu. In other words, you had to first know Telugu to learn Hindi. I lasted one week, never making it past 'Mera nam Grace.' It was pure magic that Indra and I were able to communicate at all.

It was September, the height of monsoon season. I was deflated by daily trips throughout known and obscure parts of the city, dodging the heavy rains, looking at apartments, and negotiating the rental price with landlords, only to have them turn me down in the end. I had thought that my American dollars, and the fact that I could offer three months' rent in advance, would be enough. I was wrong. Landlords didn't want to rent to me—a single woman, in her twenties, with no family attachments in sight. 'You're suspicious to them,' I was told one night by well-meaning Indians at a dinner welcoming me and other Fulbright Fellows to India. 'You're a young Indian woman, you have no husband, no father, no male relative with you, and you're asking to rent an apartment for yourself. Women just don't do that here. Women don't live alone here.'

I finally did find a flat, in a noisy and dusty residential enclave in downtown Hyderabad known as Begumpet, not far from the city's airport. The two-bedroom, third floor flat had been previously occupied by a fellow American Fulbright Fellow—as luck would have it, his Fulbright year was up, and I, thankfully, could move in and take his place. This was how I met Indra.

He shared that there was a woman who came to the flat every day at noon—she cleaned the apartment, washed the clothes, did the dishes, bought the groceries, and cooked lunch. He asked me to keep her employed. I knew that a culture of servitude, of having women, sometimes very young girls, working as servants, was a norm for many homes in India. I didn't want to be part of this. So, I initially refused, not just because of my feelings about the ethics of this practice but also because I was convinced I would be fine creating a life in Hyderabad on my own.

I would be wrong. I had never lived by myself before. I was piloting being on my own for the first time at twenty-two years old in a foreign land where I knew no one and barely spoke just one of the country's multiple languages. And so, I reconsidered, I needed Indra more than Indra needed me.

Indra worked from eight o'clock in the morning to twelve noon in the apartment on the ninth floor of the building, and from twelve to three o'clock in my flat. I learned later that there was a third family she worked for from late afternoon into the evening. This was Indra's day—cleaning, washing, and cooking for three households from eight o'clock in the morning to eight o'clock at night—before she made it back to her own home to make dinner for her husband and two children.

Indra might have been younger, but she looked like she was in her fifties. A life of toil and labor had ungracefully aged her. Later, she would share with me that she wasn't sure how old she was. She had no birth certificate. No official documents marked her coming into this world. No papers claimed her as a citizen of India. Her mother and father passed away when she was a little girl. All she knew was that, from the time she was born, she had spent all her days in Hyderabad.

With Indra's daily presence in the flat my Hindi expanded—mostly with the language of food. Every week, she shopped for groceries and ran through a list of what she would get:

> baiṅgana—eggplant
> kaddū—pumpkin
> ālū—potato
> gōbhī—cabbage
> phūlagōbhī—cauliflower
> bhiṇḍī—okra

Indra curried everything she cooked. She treated garlic and ginger like they were pepper, with an overzealous dash of each. Every meal came with the trifecta of rice, dahl, and chappatis. She was a master of Indian cuisine. Although I might have been having a semblance of the same meal every day, I was given a feast.

I never gave Indra any requests about what to do around the flat. I wouldn't have been able to communicate instructions anyway. Also, I didn't take well to being Indra's boss, in fact, I was quite resistant to it. I had grown up hearing the stories my grandmother, my father's mother, told as she too cared for other women's homes. She took great pride in the excellence of her work. But it pained her to labor over making another woman's home beautiful every day, when she couldn't do the same for her own. Granny Doris never had a home of her own. She spent most of her life as a squatter, living in a makeshift shack on someone's else's property in Georgetown that, any day, could have been razed. Eventually it was. She left her home each morning knowing that when she returned at night it might not be there. To protect herself from losing the thing that was the deepest desire of her heart—a home of her own—she lived in total detachment of the shack. For Granny Doris, her home was a place to lay her head at night. But she poured all her might, muscle, and creativity into making other women's homes sparkle.

Because of my grandmother, I was sensitive to Indra's role. I was no mistress of the house. I left that title exclusively to Indra. I had given her a set of keys and she decided how, when, and what things needed to be done. She dictated what to cook, what groceries to buy, and how many rupees were needed for it all. For the year I lived there, the flat was as much Indra's as it was mine. Often, when I would leave town to attend some academic conference, Indra and her children chose to stay in the flat. I would return a week or so later and find the bed untouched. The straw mats Indra brought from her home were rolled up and set aside in a corner of the living room. While I was gone, she and her children slept on the floor.

I never saw Indra write anything down. Never saw her put pen to paper. I suspected that she could not read or write. But I never asked as I was worried the question would invade her privacy. She would light up, however, when I brought home brown paper bags filled with notebooks and pencils for Manju, her little girl. Manju and I shared a similar love—the sacred act of opening up a new notebook and writing on its first crisp page. She greeted every new notebook with delicacy. She opened it slowly, ran her palm across the first page, and pulled it to her nose to take in the scent of its newness. And she thought carefully about what would grace the first page. Precocious Manju talked circles around both her mother and me. At ten years old, she was learning Hindi, Telugu, and English in school. She filled up a lot of notebooks.

My relationship with Indra evolved without any direction or intent that it ought to do so. Soon, I couldn't imagine India without Indra. When, toward the end of the monsoon season, I fell dangerously ill with a tropical flu, it was she who stripped my fevered body, sponged me down with warm water as if bathing a child, and fashioned a homemade poultice for my chest. Two weeks later and mending, I still couldn't hold any real food down and had lost nearly ten pounds. Indra would bring from her own kitchen tiffins steaming with broth. 'Kana Kana!' she would urge. 'Eat, eat,' her tone at once soothing, at once worried, and as usual, bossy. In my weeks of illness, she was not to be questioned. In her formidability I saw why she was named for the Hindu god of thunder.

Soon, I was back to my routine again, spending mornings and early afternoons on the campus at the University of Hyderabad. Professionally, as a Fulbright Fellow, I was researching how Indian women's literature impacted the movement for women's equal rights. Privately, I went to India to find a connection to the women whose Indian names I did not carry. I am part of a lineage of women—my grandmothers Doris and Inez, my mother Ingrid, my sister Candace—with names far removed from India, our motherland and from Hindi, our mother tongue. Yet, when you look at us, we are clearly India's women; our roots tangled up in India's soil. Months into my research, I was feeling more and more lost, overwhelmed by the complexities and contradictions in the notion of equality for women and girls in a country that everyday continued to baffle me. And I was riddled with self-doubt, confronted with insecurities. Why did I think I was qualified to take on this kind of work? How could I, with all my privilege, possibly understand the lives of the women here?

The days I came back to the flat, and Indra had some extra time before she left for her third job, were the times we ate a late lunch together and where I fussed about her eating on the floor. She would arrange two robust plates with the different vegetables she had curried for the day and a nice helping of rice and dahl, warm the chappatis on the tawa on the kerosene stove, and make a fresh batch of cold nimboo pani—the juice from freshly squeezed limes shaken with water, cayenne pepper, and a little bit of sugar. I relished the ceremonious way Indra treated the act of preparing and plating a meal. She embraced food as sacred. She, in turn, would fuss at me if I brought a book to the meal. She scolded me: when you eat, you must only eat. For Indra, mealtime was a gift. It deserved one's full presence.

With her plate and cup filled, she would stoop to the linoleum floor, balancing them with precision as she descended. Indra sat on the floor, because as a Dalit, a woman of India's untouchable caste, she wasn't permitted to sit at the table with me. Considered tainted and impure, she was forbidden to share in the meal she lovingly labored over for us. Indra ate from the same steel tiffin plate and cup every time. She wouldn't share the same plates, cups, forks or spoons that I used. She would wash her plate and cup and leave it to dry in its own segregated corner of the dish rack where it did not touch the other kitchen wares. Despite my gestures, my urging of 'nahī, nahī' in Hindi each time she descended to the floor, Indra always refused. For her, the matter was bigger than sitting on the floor. She was a woman who abided by the values of her culture, privately and publicly. She did so without question, without temptation. Her resistance to me was her submission—to what she believed in, to what was instilled in her.

As the year lingered on, I continued to spend my days immersed in my research on Indian women's history through dramatic titles such as *The Legally Dispossessed*, *Enslaved Daughters*, and *Death by Fire*. And in the afternoons, I came home to Indra, to our lunch ceremony, to our quiet dance between the table and the floor. There with Indra was where I learned about the women of India. There with Indra was where I found my education.

ARRIVAL
8 October 2010
Chaffee Jenetta, Deder District, Momicha Rural Village, Ethiopia

The Girl with the Notebook

There were no paved roads directly to Chaffee Jenetta. Telephone lines and electric wires were rare in those parts. Women were immersed in their day—fetching water, gathering wood and sticks to stoke fires, and cooking for their families. In this small Muslim coffee farming community nestled in the remote terrains of Eastern Ethiopia, I found comfort in the company of lush mountains and endless blue sky.

The journey to Chaffee Jenetta had started over a year ago in Harlem, New York where I called home. I was invited to travel with the board members of an NGO that works with coffee planters in Ethiopia's rural villages, helping them to grow better coffee and earn higher incomes. I had been supporting their fundraising and outreach efforts through their Harlem office and was drawn to the organization's model of enlisting the support of these farmers to improve social services in Chaffee Jenetta like clinics, schools, and access to clean water.

It was my first time in Ethiopia and my first trip to Africa. I learned from a previous year of traveling throughout India that there was no preparing for the rural countryside. You simply showed up and let the land lead. I embraced Ethiopia with the same deference. While our group assessed the farming conditions and needs of the village, I spent most of the time with the school children. I had learned that as early as nine years old, Chaffee Jenetta's children began working on the coffee farms to help support their families. A girl, about nine or ten years old, caught my attention. I asked for her name, but she was too shy to tell me. I pointed to the books she clutched under her arm and asked if I could look at them. Her notes, written in Oromo, the local language of Chaffee Jenetta, filled up every usable blank space. Her handwriting was in the margins, on the inside and outside of the covers, written horizontally and vertically.

I recalled my own primary school days growing up in Guyana when notebooks and paper were a luxury. We used them sparingly and only for important schoolwork. Instead, we had hand-held chalkboards and little bits of chalk. It was cheaper, but it meant everything that was written had to be erased. I wanted to be a writer. I would gather sheets of paper wherever I could find them and glue or sew them together to make books. It was within those pages that I could invent the life I wanted.

When my grandmother and aunts noticed this little hobby of mine, I quickly became their official reader and writer. Letters arrived from relatives living in the United States, Canada, or England, and I was asked to read them aloud and help write the response. That many of the women in my family struggled to read was normal to me. It never struck me as unusual that they relied on me to transcribe intimate details about their lives. Perhaps, this is why I wrote so guardedly in my own notebooks—I knew privacy was a privilege.

Like that little girl in Chaffee Jenetta, I left no free space unmarked in my hand-made books. I too wrote in the margins, within the covers, and sideways. I wondered if this was where the stories of Chaffee Jenetta were being kept. Were they scribbled within the margins? Were they tucked in between the covers?

One of the Ethiopian guides that accompanied our group remarked, 'These are the forgotten people.' He had never been this deep into the mountains of the Deder District either and was visibly moved by the agrarian way of life in Chaffee Jenetta. Perhaps what he was witnessing made him feel as a foreigner in his own land.

But as I stood there looking through this little girl's notebooks, nothing about her seemed forgotten to me. There was a boldness about her. There was a joyfulness about her. What I saw was a young girl thriving amidst her circumstances. I've found this to be universal—people thriving amidst contradictions, thriving in the messiness of life, thriving in the tragedies, thriving in the challenges, the hurts and the disappointments.

Notebooks may seem trivial when compared to the serious needs in Chaffee Jenetta like clean water, clinics, and paved roads. But they represent the freedom to dream, to create, and to imagine a future for oneself. For that little girl, her future begins within the pages of her notebook—just as my dreams began for me. It was clear by the way she clung to her books, its pale blue covers tattered and torn, that what was written in them was of value. They were sacred to her.

The more I thought about our Ethiopian guide's words that these were 'forgotten people' the more it unsettled me. Far too often the narratives about women and girls in rural communities whether they be in Asia, or Africa, or South America, or the Caribbean, are centered on an urgent call to look past the proverbial courtyard, to aim for a life beyond the confines of the village, to shed the veil. And we tell them that not doing so would render them invisible, marginalized, or trapped. We're wrong. Chaffee Jenetta is not another nameless village in another ubiquitous story of poverty in Africa. It is a unique place, a challenging place, a wealthy place—albeit not material wealth. It is not a place to flee from, but one to be nourished and supported.

The little girl I met could turn out to be a powerful voice for Ethiopia—her Ethiopia, no one else's. She might one day become a writer herself, sharing with the world its multiple stories. And to do so, perhaps she will find herself returning to those very notebooks. She could light the world.

The Ones Who Leave . . . the Ones Who Are Left

Twenty years after I left Guyana, I returned for the first time in 2014. I reunited with V, my first best friend. My last best friend. It was a 100-degrees or so it felt. Georgetown was having a Roman August. I was thankful for the desolation that left the city feeling like it belonged only to me and V. We were at a café on Main Street. That amused me because when I was growing up there in the 1980s and 90s, my family never stepped foot in cafés. We never once ate in restaurants. We couldn't afford the extravagance. We ate all of our meals at home. Everyone I knew did, too.

V told me that I hadn't changed a bit. I fibbed as well and returned the compliment. We looked at each other and giggled—we were still defending each other like best friends do. We both sat on the same side of the table, tucked close, shoulder-to-shoulder, thigh-to-thigh. We had put aside our grown-women selves for the moment and were back to being the fourteen-year-old girls we were when we'd last seen each other. Like me, V bounced around in dresses always bright and floral and flowing. The Pentecostal church on Middle Road where our families attended, where our friendship began and flourished, was strict about what girls had to wear—skirts and dresses at least one inch below the knees. No pants, no jeans, no shorts, no tights, ever. Pants were for boys and men. No makeup nor jewelry. The slightest hint of color on your lips and you were branded Jezebel. Although my adult brain now knew those definitions of piety and chaste were extreme, they still kept a strong hold. It's why it took me until I was thirty-two years old and a whole continent between me and the Pentecostal church, to pierce my ears.

Though I never told her, I was always a little jealous of V. Of all the little brown-skin Indian girls in the church, I thought she was the prettiest. The church boys agreed, too. While I remained delicate and thin, V embraced the changes in the contours of her body with grace and confidence. She was brilliant. She was a master multi-tasker. I was singular in my vision: church and school. V had what my skinny, bookish, timid self didn't—presence and personality. She was beautiful, and she was popular. None of which I was. I kept my envy in check and clung to her with the hopes that some of her boldness and popularity would rub off on me for my own good.

I spent a lot of time in her bottom house flat. For our Saturday afternoon ritual, I made the ten-minute walk from the end of Middle Road where I lived, passing by the church, to the top of the road, where V lived. My whole life existed on Middle Road—my house, my church, my best friend—and that's all I needed. In my fourteen years of living in Guyana, we moved four times, and yet we never left Middle Road. V's house was always immaculately clean. Everything in it had its proper place. More like its proper alignment—it had to be angled just a certain way. Her mother was Feng Shui-ing in Guyana before it was a global trend. It's easy to be a minimalist when you don't have much to begin with. V's tiny two-room house was an oasis compared to my equally tiny but crowded and messy bottom house flat. My mother readily admitted that organization was not her thing.

V was always loyal to me with her secrets. There were many Saturday nights when we huddled near the glow of the kerosene lamp at her kitchen table under the darkness of the city's blackout where we were supposed to do homework or memorize another New Testament book for Sunday school the next morning. Instead, we gossiped, shared our crushes on the boys in church, planned our weddings. This sharing of our interior world sealed our friendship.

V's house felt safe and warm. I often wished I had V's family. Her father, a kind, soft-spoken man, never walked out on her mother. I had too many memories of begging my daddy to stay.

When I left Guyana and I left V, we both made promises. We would write each other every month. We would send pictures. I would come back to Guyana once a year. I never wrote and I never went back. As I sat next to her in the café twenty years later, I found myself staring at her face as if she was some long-lost lover and I was trying to determine if the loving feeling was still there. I wondered if she forgave me for leaving her.

I had no knowledge of what had happened in her life since I climbed the stairs to my Guyana Airways one-way flight bound for JFK. I've since been on many planes and gone through a few passports filled up with multiple immigration stamps. V has never left Guyana. She has no passport with its pages marked with official stamps of the places she's been. A passport, or the absence of one, becomes a symbol of how two lives that begin together, diverge.

When the waitress at the café came over and asked for our lunch order, I predictably chose the chicken and potato curry with rice, and sliced cucumbers and pepper sauce on the side. V ordered a Coca-Cola in the can. I asked if she wasn't hungry. She told me she still doesn't eat restaurant food.

In a silly attempt to be funny, I said to her, 'Tell me everything that's happened in the last twenty years and start from the beginning.' This turned out to be a serious request for V. It wasn't funny to her. She left me in girlhood and shifted to womanhood. She began with facts and chronology. She told me she married early. She was the mother of two children and had left the physically violent and abusive marriage. She and her two babies were now living back in the house on Middle Road with her father. She told me she had no money and no job.

I was in awe of how she could summarize twenty years into Polaroid snapshots. Throughout V's retelling, I felt my presence at the table slowly fading. This was not the homecoming nor reunion I imagined. I didn't know what to do with the things I was being told, other than it seemed necessary to V that I know them, that I hear her. V was unwavering and stoic in her reporting. She would make a fine journalist. I could picture her giving a briefing from the belly of a ravaged, war-torn land. She would be unflinching in her delivery of the facts—the body counts, the wreckage.

As V continued her story, I realized it was me who remained in girlhood. It was me for whom time stopped. When she reached the part of her story of the physical abuse she'd endured for years, it was the part that broke me and brought on my tears. I visualized those scenes, and in them I didn't see the thirty-three-year-old woman sitting next to me, I saw my fourteen-year-old best friend. And yet, V was not distracted by my tears. She was not moved. She did not partake in my outrage or in my devastation or in my sadness over what had transpired in her life since we last saw each other as girls. She knew that my tears were not about her.

My tears were about my own guilt: Is this what happens to the ones who are left? To the girls who can't leave? My tears were about my own gratitude. This is what could have happened to me. Sitting next to me was my best friend, telling me about the life I too should have had. There it was, the two agonies of guilt and gratitude, tucked close, hand in hand.

When V finished her Coca-Cola and her story, she told me she couldn't stay much longer because she had to get back to her babies. A neighbor was watching them. From my bag, I reached for the small envelope I had prepared for her before coming to the café. In it were American dollars and a copy of an old photograph—the image of me as a girl when she last saw me. It is one of the handful of photographs my family brought to the United States with us that I keep preserved—with the other relics of the self I left behind in another country—in a large rustic blue-linen box in my Manhattan apartment. I didn't have a single photograph of the two of us together. I wanted to give this copy to V because it marked the moment when nothing had yet changed in our lives. We didn't know those were our last days together. We were yet to be defined by the categories of the girl who leaves and the girl who is left. Behind the photograph, I had written her a note. One of the lines said, 'Whenever I think of Guyana, I always think of you.'

After V's story, those lines were now burdened with a new sordid meaning that they didn't have when I penned them. I was cringing at how they seemed so trite, so naïve, so unworthy of the moment. Worse, so self-indulgent. They were all the wrong words. I didn't know what the right ones ought to be. I slipped the photograph out of the envelope, leaving only the money, and handed it to V. She peeked at the fifty-dollar bills, and without saying anything, quickly put it in her purse. Neither I nor V suggested that we take a photograph of the two of us reunited after twenty years.

Neither of us felt compelled to memorialize the moment. V never asked about my life in the past twenty years. She didn't request that I too start from the beginning of our moment of departure. She knew that in two days, I would get on another plane, I would have another stamp in the pages in my American passport. I would leave, again.

Author's Note

The essay's title, 'The Geography of Separation,' is inspired by a line from the poem 'From the Book of Mothers,' by Jamaican-American poet Shara McCallum, in which she asks, 'What is separation's geography?' (Shara McCallum, *This Strange Land* (Farmington, ME: Alice James Books, 2011), p. 60). The essay is a work of creative nonfiction. Where I deemed it necessary, I have changed names, details, and determining characteristics of certain people, places, or events to avoid compromising anyone's privacy.

5.

Transplantation

—

Dominique Hunter

Figure 5.1
Dominique Hunter, 'You Will Find Solace Here'
2016, digital collage.

    https://doi.org/10.11647/OBP.0218.07

Transplantation

/ˌtransplɑːnˈteɪʃ(ə)n, tranzplɑːnˈteɪʃ(ə)n/

noun

noun: **transplantation**; plural noun: **transplantations**

1. the process of taking an organ or living tissue and implanting it in another part of the body or in another body.

2. the movement or transfer of someone or something to another place or situation.

This is the result of a Google search for 'transplantation definition,' the first of more than eleven million results to appear at the top of the webpage. It identifies two distinct and seemingly unrelated examples of word usage. There is no overlap in the way they are presented.

But perhaps they are not as disconnected as we are led to believe. Perhaps there exists a scenario in which the two are sister components, two leaves on the same branch of the same tree. Hearts, minds, souls, eyes, and feet continuously moving through real and abstract bodies and spaces that are both ours and the other. All the while tethered to our individual sources like umbilical cords.

Broken down to their most essential elements both speak of body and movement. Consider for a moment the many implications of that juxtaposition:

• What does it mean to be actively engaged in both processes of transplantation?

• How does it influence the nuances of our migration patterns, if at all?

• Is it possible to shift around parts of our bodies as needed, reanimating broken organs as we move through obscure places, fending off threats to our wellness and bias for self-preservation?

Some would call us immigrants, movers across borders that are not our own. We are, each of us, a body and a tree, flexible and fixed. Years of shapeshifting have strengthened the muscles that accommodate our steady transition between these two states of being. So, we persist. We do not give much thought to this back and forth, this act of going and coming, uprooting and transplanting. It is simply what we do. It is what we have always done, all of us, in some way. That is our history and it is our future. Ours is a collection of personal truths forever intertwined with the perplexing tendrils of shifting roots.

A Guide to Surviving Transplantation and Other Traumas

Make a general assessment of the land.

We imagine fantastic opportunities promising to rip us away from the poverty/obscurity/mediocrity/lawlessness that threaten to hold hostage our potential. Tangled weeds shoot up, wild and indiscriminate, mocking that twisted nature, pushing past weary fences. We have inherited the impetus to push back long before the water and sun release us from our hardened selves.

Identify a strategic point of entry.

My own breakthrough to adulthood was marked by a contradictory sequence of hesitation and urgency. Mine was not a shell made of the same substance as my parents. And while this 'new' national climate of opportunity that coaxed me out of said shell was far from ideal, it was, in many ways, more sympathetic to my deficiencies. My form being pliable and therefore much more vulnerable than theirs, meant that I had to adopt new ways of strengthening those shortcomings to avoid complacency.

Clear a path with a pair of long boots.

Like all good nurturers my parents toiled so that I would somehow be exempt from the jabs thrown by life in what we embrace as our 'third world' country, despite the growing global debates about this term. Admittedly, many struggles have escaped me. But the challenge of finding and sustaining a creative self was and will always be mine alone to shoulder. Many battles have been fought both on and off the field that never forgets. It was through rigorous trial and error that I came to discover my own footpath, hidden under the darkness of the Georgetown sky.

Prepare the ground for easy transition.

How much further can a potted plant grow? How many moons until we crash against the impenetrable glass ceiling of that cramped reality? How long until our own roots, too thick to be contained, choke our potential to death? We plateau, before making our way downward, forced deep into a kind of cold and indifferent new ground. We know indifference. But this is, at the same time, familiar and alien, an opportunity and an unlikelihood. Nevertheless, we push through, hoping for a better place than the one we left behind.

Figure 5.2
Dominique Hunter, 'Contemplating Strategies'
2017, digital collage.

© Dominique Hunter. Courtesy of the artist. CC BY-NC-ND.

Select the healthiest candidates for the highest success rate.

Our greatest aspiration should be to leave. This is what we are told, even as tiny buds still growing in our mothers' bellies. Broken sermons recount dismal days gone and predict even darker days to come. That is our oral tradition, an enduring account of desolation perpetuated equally by those who have stayed and those who have left. Everyone knows the single story. How can we not know it when we have grown in its shadow? There is an expectation once you have reached a certain age: pack what you can and leave. I am well past that age, yet I remain, stubbornly rooted in the land my parents spent all of their lives cultivating.

Keep the roots moist before removing.

I know very little of my parents' ancestry, the distances they traveled, the places they settled. The few stories I have heard were shared on rare occasions, long after I had reached the appropriate age to engage in 'big people story.' It was common knowledge at the time that a child dare not entertain the thought of questioning his/her elders. That was not a child's place. Regardless, my imagination ran wild with thoughts of the two very distinct lines of African and Indian heritage in my family, and the point of intersection that ultimately led to me.

Remove from the original container.

Years later I had sensed there might have been a great deal of pain behind the recounting of those stories, so I never probed beyond the bits of information they volunteered. I knew the tension between races was much thicker than it is today but I could not fathom what that meant for an Indian man and his Black wife in those times. I could not imagine navigating a field wired with explosives, ready to burst open and claim lives at any moment. But perhaps it was best not to look back. I suspected, too, that a lot had been inadvertently forgotten in the years since. Most of the persons with concrete knowledge about either side of my family had left this realm years ago, taking with them the answers to questions regarding the history of the people whose DNA I share.

Transfer to new ground.

I knew there was Dutch ancestry as my maternal great grandmother had traveled from Dutch Guiana (now Suriname) to British Guiana. What brought her here was anyone's guess, but it could not have been very far off the usual driving force: betterment. Very little else is known about her family prior to her migration to British Guiana. Within Guyana's borders, my mother and father's family covered quite a lot of ground. My mother grew up in a mining village known as 111 Miles Mahdia, Potaro (Region 8). My father's immediate family, on the other hand, spent their formative years in the mining town of Kwakwani in the Upper Demerara-Berbice region. While his mother was originally from Plaisance, East Coast Demerara, his father's roots extended as far as Skeldon, East Berbice Corentyne.

Careful planting is essential for root development.

Every chance that presents itself, people would ask, 'What is wrong with you?' While most would spring at the opportunity to leave Guyana, I have never felt compelled to move, at least not permanently. This marks the difference between my travel patterns and those of my ancestors. Home is where the metaphorical 'navel string' is buried. Mine is buried along Guyana's coastal plain, deep beneath years of treasured memories and idyllic dreamscapes. I could not imagine leaving entirely unless I felt the cold, hard rock of failure pressed against my back, with nothing and no one left to tie me to the only home I have ever known. Plaisance, Campbellville, Blygezight Gardens, Guyana.

Stake the young to avoid root damage.

Still, how does one not shrink in the face of ever-present poverty/obscurity/mediocrity/lawlessness? Those who choose to stay in spite of everything must find ways to circumvent the grinding down of our resolve. We take refuge in the things and places that dull the harshness of reality, forgetting momentarily the blight of our anxieties. There is a kind of mulishness in the way we refuse to buckle under the weight of our choice to stay. We have learned to maneuver comfortably between familiarity and contempt a long time ago.

Figure 5.3
Dominique Hunter, 'Black Water Remedy'
2016, digital collage.

Add sugar solution to prevent shock.

The way we move through various spaces is not something we are conscious of until the enlightened observer mentions it. In fact, prior to this there had been no serious consideration of my own actions, the constant advancing from and retreating to a very specific epicenter. Footprints in the earth extending a bit further each time but, ultimately, always leading back to its place of origin. How far will this magical cord extend before yielding its elasticity to overuse? What will be the coordinates of my final stop when the cord can stretch no more? Will the sun still burn my skin with the same intensity?

Spread compost around the base for additional nutrients.

It is difficult to imagine the energy required to fuel that kind of regular transplantation. In much the same way, it is difficult for me to describe the mental and physical tax exacted during my weekly retreats to the countryside and less frequent trips overseas. Nevertheless, these 'mini migrations' have become central to the maintenance of my overall mental health and, by extension, the integrity of every other faculty of my body. They are equally responsible for the continued growth of my creative practice as well as the expansion of my network. Like vines that crawl along the chain-linked fence of my family's country home, I will spend the rest of my days chasing the fleeting light.

Water regularly but not excessively.

This constant extraction process, although exhausting and violent, is a necessary routine for my contemporaries and me. In response, we have learned to steel ourselves against the trauma of that ripping action in an effort to curtail the initial shock of change. Our knowledge of trauma runs deep. How can we not know it so intimately when this land and its peoples have been forged by its ferocity? Our country has survived in spite of violent racism, dirty politics, bloody massacres, and crazed cult leaders who have stained our soil in a most tragic red the spectrum could ever generate. These are hardly new phenomena. We endure. We survive. In a rather perverse way, trauma is one of our more faithful companions.

Make available the right amount of sunlight.

We challenge ourselves to make those treks daily, weekly, monthly, determined to stave off the lingering threat of disenchantment. How easy it is to lose one's sense of direction when insularity is the very soil that holds us together. That back and forth movement therefore becomes a crucial component in the way we keep ourselves sane.

The bigger picture is always in sharp focus even as we shift temporarily from one place to the next before eventually settling back into this contentious territory we call home.

Wait patiently for it to take.

In the end it matters not how painful a process it is. This is the price of not leaving. The cost is shouldered willingly if it means we can have it both ways. We wait in the shade of old trees for the next opportunity that would allow for the occasional dipping of our roots in a body of water that is not ours.

Repeat steps as needed.

6.

Those Who Remain:
Portraits of Amerindian Women

—

Khadija Benn

Guyanese have long experienced family separations through transnational migration, mainly to bordering countries, the Caribbean, North America, and the United Kingdom. Labor migration has been a key driver of outward movement from Guyana. Its effects are particularly evident in indigenous communities as Amerindians transition to new countries in pursuit of gainful employment. Yet, many family members often remain. The seldom explored stories of indigenous people who choose not to migrate offer valuable insights on their notions of propinquity.

I encountered the women—the maternal elders of their families—featured in this photo essay while conducting research on social vulnerability in Guyana's interior. As a geographer my work involves settlement mapping and community-level assessments, and photography helps me to inform this practice. In our conversations on their lived experiences at the villages, they recalled family members who resettled in other countries and shared with me how they stay connected—along with the difficulties of doing so. These dialogues surfaced their unique perceptions of time and space and revealed that distance is largely viewed as a relative construct that is immaterial against their strong ancestral ties. For instance, many did not perceive relatives living in neighboring countries as having settled 'abroad,' as Amerindians have traditionally considered these international borders as fluid.

Their stories convey concerns on how migration contributes to loss of traditional cultures, languages, and communal ways of life. But those threats are succeeded by the dignity and resilience of those who remain. These intimate portraits underscore Guyana's rich Amerindian narrative and emphasize the role of matriarchs in shaping the lives of the next generation—regardless of where they end up—sustained by their heritage, traditional values, and work ethic, and anchored by a profound connection with their lands.

    https://doi.org/10.11647/OBP.0218.08

'Even though so many of them gone, this is my country . . .
I couldn't be happier being home in Guyana.'

Anastacia Winters was born in the Wapichan village of Maruranau and eventually settled in Lethem, the Region's administrative center, in the 1970s. She worked at the Lethem Hospital for many years while caring for her six children. Today, several of her relatives—two sisters, a niece, a son, and a stepson—live in the neighboring Brazilian settlements of Bon Fim and Boa Vista. Anastacia explained that their decision to migrate was based on the need to access wider employment prospects than what was available in Guyana at the time. Occasionally they visit home, and she sees them often when she travels to Brazil. Another niece who has resided in the United States for more than twenty-five years calls home dutifully every week. Despite the throes of migration, Anastacia's family has managed to remain close, which she attributes to the strong familial values sustained by her tribe.

Figure 6.1
Anastacia Winters *(b. 1947)*

Lethem, Upper Takutu-Upper Essequibo (Region Nine), Guyana. Khadija Benn, 'Anastacia Winters', from the series 'Those Who Remain: Portraits of Amerindian Women', 2017, digital photography.

'Everybody is here, my children, my grandchildren . . . this is where I belong.'

Mickilina Simon was born in Sand Creek Village, a Wapichan settlement in central Rupununi, where she planted crops such as cassava, banana, pineapples, and sugar cane to sustain her family. Mickilina now lives in Lethem with her son and granddaughter, moving there many years ago to help raise her grandchildren. Her six children all live in Guyana, but she has one close niece who migrated to Brazil in the late nineties. They maintained a close relationship over the years, talking regularly on the phone and visiting each other for weeks at a time. Mickilina says she was never interested in moving to north Brazil despite spending considerable time there and experiencing firsthand a more modern way of life. While learning the Portuguese language is a key deterring factor for her (she is fluent in both English and Wapichana), Mickilina asserts that she prefers the slower, simpler pace in her corner of Guyana.

Figure 6.2
Mickilina Simon *(b. 1938)*

*Tabatinga, Lethem, Upper Takutu-Upper Essequibo (Region Nine), Guyana. Khadija Benn, 'Mickilina Simon', from the series
'Those Who Remain: Portraits of Amerindian Women', 2017, digital photography.*

'I tell people that I born and grow in Guyana, and I will die in Guyana. I like to walk; I like to be free.'

Lillian Singh spent her entire life in Toka, a quiet Macushi village in the upper Rupununi Savannahs. She lives there with her mother, husband, and two youngest children, and farms peanuts, corn, and bitter cassava. As is characteristic of Amerindian families, Lillian is close with extended family members. When she was eight years old, her aunt migrated to nearby Venezuela and her great-uncle moved to Brazil. They often visited Toka but age now prevents them from traveling. These days Lillian makes the occasional trip across the borders to spend time with them. She also related how one of her sons migrated in 2000 to Boa Vista, where he found work as a vaquero on a cattle ranch. Eventually he moved deeper into Brazil with his two children after his wife passed away. She explained that she lost touch with them after that move, as her village did not have telecommunication services in those days. She hasn't heard from them in many years but remains hopeful that someday they will be able to reconnect.

Figure 6.3
Lillian Singh *(b. 1962)*

Toka, North Rupununi, Upper Takutu-Upper Essequibo (Region Nine), Guyana. Khadija Benn, 'Lillian Singh', from the series 'Those Who Remain: Portraits of Amerindian Women', 2017, digital photography.

Violet James settled in Almond Beach in the 1980s when her husband undertook work as a sea turtle warden and conservationist. The small Almond Beach community sits at the northernmost point of the Shell Beach Protected Area, a 145 km stretch of coastland that is a vital nesting ground for four endangered marine turtle species. Of Violet's seven children, three live abroad—a son and daughter live in the United States, and a daughter lives in Venezuela. Limited telecommunications at the remote Shell Beach location challenged Violet's ability to keep in touch with her children, and she has heard from her daughter less in recent years as the situation worsened in Venezuela. She is proud that some of her children had the opportunity to leave Guyana but wishes she could speak with them more. While she doesn't expect to see them regularly in the future, Violet expressed that even though migration places so much time and distance between them, she will continue to remain close with her children.

Figure 6.4
Violet James *(b. 1952)*

Almond Beach, Barima-Waini (Region One), Guyana. Khadija Benn, 'Violet James', from the series 'Those Who Remain: Portraits of Amerindian Women', 2017, digital photography.

Figure 6.5

Violet James sifts rice with her neighbor in a traditional detached kitchen. Khadija Benn, *Violet James*, from the series *Those Who Remain: Portraits of Amerindian Women*, 2017, digital photography.

Figure 6.6

Surrounded by mementos in her living room, Lucille Beaton glances at the barrel sent by her son, who resides in Canada. Khadija Benn, *Lucille Beaton*, from the series *Those Who Remain: Portraits of Amerindian Women*, 2017, digital photography.

Lucille Beaton grew up at the Barama River mouth and eventually settled in Mabaruma, the northernmost town in Guyana. She spent most of her life fishing, farming, and raising her eight children. Most of her children still reside in Guyana, but she rarely sees them as their relationships have become strained over the years. Her closest bond is with one son who has lived in Canada for most of his adult life. Lucille was overjoyed when he had the opportunity many years ago to leave Guyana and make a better life for himself. Since leaving he has only visited home twice. She no longer remembers how much time has passed since he moved away, but she still misses him daily. He continues to support her, and they share regular phone calls. Alone in her simple wooden home, Lucille says she was never inclined to leave Guyana. She now occupies her days with activities for her church, where she has found solace and a deep sense of community.

Figure 6.7
Lucille Beaton *(b. 1937)*

Mabaruma, Barima-Waini (Region One), Guyana. Khadija Benn, 'Lucille Beaton', from the series 'Those Who Remain: Portraits of Amerindian Women', 2017, digital photography.

Agnes Phang was born in Mabaruma and has lived much of her life there. As a mother of fourteen children, her earlier days were spent subsistence farming and caring for her children. Many of them went on to raise their own families, some doing so further away than others. Agnes related how one of her daughters migrated to Venezuela more than thirty years ago. She has visited her daughter's home a few times, but her grandchildren have never visited Guyana and she is unable to converse with them as they grew up learning Spanish. Agnes also has a sister living in England with whom she maintains a fond relationship. She has traveled to England several times to visit her, and her sister returns to Mabaruma about once a year to visit relatives and maintain the family property. Agnes says her travels to visit with family have allowed her to experience many interesting places, but she loves her home in Mabaruma above all others.

Figure 6.8
Agnes Phang *(b. 1940)*

Mabaruma, Barima-Waini (Region One), Guyana. Khadija Benn, 'Agnes Phang', from the series 'Those Who Remain: Portraits of Amerindian Women', 2017, digital photography.

'I never want to live anywhere else ... but it would be nice to see how [my children] living now.'

Yvonne Gomes grew up in Morawhanna, which was once a vibrant fishing and farming village situated near the Barima estuary. In the late 1980s frequent floods from increased tidal events forced her family to relocate to nearby Mabaruma where she attended primary school as a child. Thirty years on, Yvonne is a farmer, tailor, and mother to eleven children. Over time her family unit grew smaller as some children went in search of greener pastures. More than ten years have passed since one of her daughters left Guyana to work in Barbados, and three sons migrated to work in Canada, Venezuela, and Suriname. Yvonne understood they needed to leave to secure better jobs, but she says it was hard to watch them go. As they are seldom able to travel home, the family now relies on telephones to stay in touch. Yvonne is open to traveling someday to visit her family members; but as echoed by other women in this narrative, she knows no other home, and is content to spend her remaining years in Guyana.

Figure 6.9
Yvonne Gomes *(b. 1957)*

Mabaruma, Barima-Waini (Region One), Guyana. Khadija Benn, 'Yvonne Gomes', from the series 'Those Who Remain: Portraits of Amerindian Women', 2017, digital photography.

7.

When They Left

—

Ingrid Griffith

Figure 7.1

The author, Ingrid Griffith (right) with her sister Dawn (left) and brother Oliver (center) in December 1968. Their maternal grandmother had taken them to Skevelair's Photo Studio in Georgetown, Guyana to pose in the church outfits their parents, who had recently migrated to the United States, had sent for Christmas.

     https://doi.org/10.11647/OBP.0218.09

It was one of the worst days of my life. I was seven years old, my sister—Dawn—was nine, and my brother—Oliver—four. My parents said we were lucky because they had gotten visas to the United States. It was 1968. The Guyanese exodus was well on its way.

We were at grandmother Adda's house in Georgetown on the veranda saying goodbye. That morning, my parents were leaving Guyana without us. They looked into our faces, planted kisses on our tears and promised they would be back for us soon. My stomach gurgled as my mother held me tight. The growling in my belly continued when my father did the same. It did not stop when he let me go. I wanted to pee but I was not going to even think about it.

The early morning was already sulfur bright and steaming hot, typical for equatorial Guyana. Dawn and Oliver were sobbing.

'Don't cry,' said my mother, as she brushed their tears away. 'This is a joyous moment.'

My father headed down the flight of stairs behind my mother carrying a little suitcase, the brown grip that had been stored under their bed. I stood on Adda's upstairs veranda trying hard to muffle the sound of my cry. I wanted to keep my promise to be a big girl and not cry so that my parents would keep theirs—that soon we would join them. Besides, I felt my grandmother's grip on my right shoulder.

I knew the day was coming for some time now. Since my parents had gotten visas for America, they kept telling us about the plan they were putting in place so things would run smoothly after they left. They arranged for the Indian man they heard of who drove kids to schools to take Dawn and me to our schools. They arranged for Jenny, our ex-landlord's daughter, to arrive at Adda's house early on school mornings to comb our hair. They had plans to keep us from missing them too much. They said that they would write to us constantly and send pictures. In America, they said, we would have a better life than we could ever have in Guyana.

Drops of pee soaked the crotch of my panty, the wetness now sticky along the insides of my legs.

I wanted to yell, 'I don't care about having a better life in America. I'm happy to just have us.'

Leaving Guyana for a better life had become a family tradition. In the early 1950s, my paternal great uncle left then British Guiana for England to study. He earned his college degree and returned to become one of Guyana's leading educators and a prominent composer. Some years later, my father's four older brothers left for England and the US and didn't come back; they had given up on the repressive colonial system that was stifling young people like them. My mother's three older brothers were lucky to secure jobs as deckhands on ships leaving British Guiana for foreign lands and eventually gave up on Guyana too, jumping ship in the UK and the US.

My eyes stayed focused on my parents as they walked the dirt passageway below. Others were fixed on them too. Someone leaving for America was more than a family affair; it was a neighborhood event.

'The youngest Griffith and his wife leavin' for the States. Ah hear any day now he and his wife going to America and ah hear dey leavin dere children wit his mudda.'

'Mrs. Greenidge daughter and she son-in law papers come tru. She told me the news at church last Satday.'

When word got around that my parents had gotten visas, family they barely knew showed up with toothy smiles and eyes full of pride.

'How dee, family? It's me, yuh great Aunt Lily. Ah hear muh family get lucky!'

They believed good luck rubs off.

*

Families like mine had once been giddy with glee about a new government led by Forbes Burnham, the leader of the People's National Congress. Sentiment was changing though. There were not enough jobs for every one and you had to either know somebody or know somebody who knew somebody; or you would get nowhere.

That morning, Adda's downstairs tenants and neighbors to the sides and back of her front house rose early to see my parents off. Children yawning wide and rubbing boo boo from their eyes made their way to front windows. Mothers and wives in thin nightgowns stood sideways at their half open front doors, waving. Fathers and husbands in half unbuttoned shirts headed outside to stretch their arms over the paling for a last handshake.

Most of those watching my parents had their own plans to leave Guyana. Some had a spouse who left to get settled first. Some had a son or a daughter overseas who, once they finished their studies and got a job, would send for the rest of the family. Some were biding time, waiting to get good news from the embassy like my parents, grateful that the family member in Canada or England or America who said they'd sponsor them had come through.

And there were those who were forever trying to get in touch with relatives overseas to petition them to put in the necessary paperwork and send for them even if the person was a distant relative.

As we stood on Adda's veranda, a sudden breeze off the Atlantic Ocean a few miles away lightened the air.

Daddy walked towards the rickety footbridge to the waiting taxi that would take him and Mammy to Timehri Airport. He kept tapping on the top pocket of his suit jacket pocket, probably checking to make sure he had the things he needed—his passport, plane ticket, some of his monthly teacher's salary he had converted into US dollars, the paper with his brother-in-law's information. My mother's eldest brother, Vernon, would meet them at JFK airport. Until they got on their feet, my parents would stay with Uncle Vernon and his family in Wyandanch, Long Island.

The taxi's engine hummed. The trip from Georgetown to Timehri Airport was a one-hour drive through winding, treacherous, unpaved roads and over unstable bridges.

Mammy looked more as if she belonged on a wedding cake than at the job she had at Swan's Laundry. Her A-line dress was a frosty shade of pink, her black pillbox hat matched her handbag and opened-toed, sling-back shoes.

'Earl and Gloria looking like the King and Queen this mawning,' said a neighbor. 'Yaw'll take care of yuh selves. And mus don't forget we back here.'

Regardless of how poor you were, what you wore on departure day had to be the best you could afford. You had to leave Guyana looking like you were already a success story.

Daddy nodded his head and continued tapping his hand on his breast pocket as he carried the single grip over the bridge towards the waiting taxicab. Sometimes my father wore a shirt with a tie to his teaching job at St. Sidwell's; the gabardine suit he wore that morning must have been stifling. My mother tilted her head up at us; tears filled her eyes. 'Mammy loves you,' she said.

My parents said that their leaving was the beginning of more good things to come in America. Our parents had downsized to a two-room flat on Albert Street, Georgetown. I don't remember the bigger flat we lived in before. Another family rented two similar rooms on the other side of a wall separating us. I remember spending most of my time when I was not at school between our two grandparents; we came to our flat as a family in the evenings. We didn't have a kitchen or a bathroom. Granny lived in the next yard. We relied on her cooking and the makeshift outdoor shower under her house. Under two loose floorboards in our flat was a white enamel posy my parents would reach for when we had to use the potty.

In America, we would have a house with a kitchen, an indoor bathroom, maybe two. We'd have our own bedroom. We would have a television set, maybe more than one. We'd have a backyard with a swing set. Leaving us behind was only temporary. It was necessary for a better future. So, they assured us.

I went over the plan in my head.

We were to live with Adda, my paternal grandmother, until our parents returned for us. We were to visit Granny, our maternal grandmother, on weekends for church. The fact that Adda and Granny could remain as anchors was another reason why my parents felt lucky. Both grandmothers lived close to each other in Georgetown. We would go to the same school and church. Our parents surmised that the familiar surroundings would make us feel less like we were being ripped away from everything we were used to.

Daddy placed their grip in the car trunk. Mammy opened the car door. I pulled away from Adda, ran halfway down the flight of steps and leaned out over the wooden bannister.

'Wait! Wait!' I said.

'Careful, Mako!' said Mammy, calling me by my nickname. 'Careful!'

'Fix your nighty, pull the nightie straps back up,' said Adda.

I bolted down the stairs. 'I want to tell you something!'

'Come back here, Ingrid!' said Adda.

My mother turned to walk back over the bridge.

'It's okay, Gloria, she's okay!' said Adda.

The car door slammed; the engine revved. I dashed across the bridge.

'Wait! Wait, I want to tell you something!'

I heard voices behind me but they were drowned by my shouted pleas.

'Wait! Wait!'

I didn't think to run as fast as I did down the street. I just did. The taxi was gaining speed. I started feeling dizzy. The road got blurry. I could no longer hold the knot in my stomach. The pee I had been holding in became an unstoppable force . . . The taxi became a dot in the distance.

My parents couldn't afford to wait.

*

'Wake up Dawn, Ingrid? Wake up! Time to get ready for school.' Adda kept tapping the metal frame of our bunk bed with the gold band on her ring finger.

'Jenny is going to be here in fifteen minutes for hair combing. Time to bathe. Who first?'

I pretended to be asleep, wanting to dream the same dream I had been having since the three of us moved into Adda's house three months earlier. In the dream, Daddy and Mammy returned to Guyana to get us and we had five minutes to pack our things to take to America. I decided to leave everything behind.

Dawn and I couldn't stop missing our parents or counting the days since they left us behind. Oliver was missing Mammy and Daddy even more. He had not yet turned school age. After our parents left, Oliver forgot all about his potty training. He would not own that he was wetting and soiling his underpants. He developed terrible allergies and sores on his legs that wouldn't heal. Adda sent him to live with Granny. We were now separated.

I wish I didn't have to be a big girl. I wish I were younger and as needy as Oliver so I, too, could live with Granny. Adda was adamant that she was the one our parents had put in charge and her job was to keep us 'whole' until our visas came. I couldn't understand what she meant by 'whole.' Did it have anything to do with the sadness I was feeling?

Adda's house was much bigger than our flat on Albert Street but it was filled with grandchildren now that all of her five sons were overseas. My siblings and I had slept with our parents in the same room of our two-room flat on Albert Street. So, it felt normal that seven of us—Dawn and I, our three cousins, Lilah, and Adda—slept in one bedroom. Lilah wasn't a blood relative but she became family when Adda took her in after her parents died.

That morning without opening my eyes I knew that Adda was dressed in one of her worn-out cotton shifts. I never saw the fresher dresses Adda said she was saving. Maybe, she didn't feel the need to wear them since she never left the house. The dresses she did wear stretched tight over the dome of her stomach and the stoop of her back, so worn that the armpits were frayed and faded. It was a safe bet that Adda was wearing the shiny black wig one of my uncle's sent from America. She never took it off, not even when she went to bed.

My sister and I had become curious about the goings-on in our new surroundings, things we had not noticed before. But looking to our grandmother for answers made us feel like pariahs and in less good standing than our cousins. I pressed my eyes closed. Awake, I was tempted to ask questions I wished I had asked my parents before they left us. Like: *Where did Adda grow up? What were her parents like? Why didn't she ever go outdoors? Why was she so suspicious?*

I could hear my responsible older sister sigh as she climbed out of the bunk bed below. I should have felt lucky to have an indoor shower just a few steps from the bedroom where I slept now. And I did. But I couldn't just jump out of bed and into the shower. There were rules. Dawn and I had to fetch our towels and underwear that were stored in the small front bedroom. My fresh panty and singlet had to be on, and my towel must cover everything between my armpits and kneecaps before I exited the shower.

I heard the water in the shower running, opened my eyes and decided to make the trip to the small front room. On the way, I noted other predictable things about the morning routine at Adda's house. My green enamel cup was already placed on the dining room table. Flies hovered around grease spots on a brown paper bag that held plaited bread and tennis rolls; the slab of butter covered on its dish melting. One fly, then another, landed on the rim of my cup filled with milk. Adda knew I didn't like milk. Not even chocolate milk.

I moved beyond the clutter in the living room towards one of the two rocking chairs near the front windows. I often sat on the right handle of the rocking chair looking up at the sky and daydreaming about my parents. Behind the rocking chair was the door to the small front bedroom that held our belongings and where Adda piled things—old newspapers, books, scraps, broken furniture, a bicycle.

So much had changed under Guyana's new independent government. Like the perfume scented Lux soap that used to sit next to the sink in Adda's dining room.

Since my parents left, there was no choice but to purchase the locally-manufactured, thick block of beige Zex soap. It had no scent. The Trout Hall brand orange juice in the small tin cans that our parents bought if we were coming down with a cold was also a thing of the past.

Forbes Burnham insisted that Guyana be self-reliant. But there were no jobs, little food, and a downward spiraling economy. By the early 1970s, Guyana was a dismal mess.

*

After school on Fridays, as planned, we went to Granny's house for the weekend. It was a tiny wood structure under a pitched zinc roof supported by six-foot high cinder block posts. Two parallel stairways on opposite sides of the house led to her front and back doors. Once, Granny had decided to take her eldest son's offer to go to America; but just to visit. She had her two daughters in Guyana who needed help. She said she had her 'lil house;' a community she counted on. America, she declared, was for young people.

Granny was a Seventh-day Adventist. By sundown on Friday, everything had to be in order. The radio was turned off. Chores stopped. Idle gossip ceased. Only prayers, scripture readings, and songs were allowed. We heard Granny singing through the open windows even before we bounded up the flight of stairs.

'Granny and Ollie missed y'all too, yuh know,' she said at the door. She held us to her bosom, kissed us on the tops of our heads. 'Go on through and settle down then come join Granny for worship.'

The smell of the meal she prepared for lunch the next day after church was reassuring. The pan with the seasoned ground beef and vegetables and the one with macaroni and cheese, my favorite, cooled on the stove near the backdoor.

The top half of Granny's back door stayed flung open until worship ended. Coconut trees swayed, their branches humming in the breeze. A kiskadee perched on a tree branch singing.

I looked over the zinc fence at the bottom flat in the next yard where we used to live. Jenny and her family still lived upstairs, but our downstairs flat stood empty. The white-washed greenheart wood was stripped of its paint, the grimy windows closed, the glass panes broken into pointy shards.

I pictured the room where we slept. Our bunkbed and parents' bed pressed together in the tight space. I remember how Dawn, Ollie, and I wouldn't stop jumping up and down on our parents' bed, not until one of us fell off and ended up crying. I remember the blue and white portable record player, the pickup Uncle Vernon sent from America. It stayed on the table that stood over the two loose floorboards we lifted to retrieve the posy. Mammy had a few small round records Uncle Vernon had also sent. She liked playing one by Aretha Franklin. Next to the table was the couch. It was there Daddy read us poems before we went to bed. My favorite was:

'*Some like bath nights but I do not. For the cold's so cold and the hot's so hot...*'

It was there he explained the letter writing plan that would keep us connected when they left for America.

But the letter writing plan was not working out on my end. Adda was censoring our letters. I couldn't tell my parents how different things were without them and why I was always sad. I couldn't tell them I hated school or that I no longer cared to eat. I wanted to tell them how much I needed to be with them. But by the time the letters were edited for proper grammar, punctuation, structure and content, all of me was taken out.

Dear Daddy and Mammy,
I miss you so much. I'm behaving at home and doing well at school.
Adda says hello. I can't wait to see you.
love and kisses
Ingrid

There came a time when there was no guarantee we would visit Granny every weekend as my parents had instructed. Dawn and I had to be on our best behavior during the week or Adda would cancel the weekend visit. What Adda said must stand. There was to be no discussion, no questioning, no talking back. Weekend visits to Granny ended. Being on my best behavior was in constant conflict with what I wanted to do. Was it the sinner in all of us Pastor at church talked about that Adda saw in me? My natural instincts were to be doubted, what I felt to be stifled. Adda saw it as setting me on the path of righteousness. I didn't know it then but Adda was a minister's daughter.

Were my parents missing us as much as we're missing them? Why haven't they kept their promise? How long is 'soon' anyway?

I wanted to ask my parents these questions but Adda wouldn't allow it.

At the primary school I attended, no one I knew had parents who were overseas. When I brought photos, my parents sent to school for my teacher and classmates to see, their eyes opened wide. I had to remind myself to pretend to feel lucky that I had parents in America.

*

The six years without my parents drew on. I witnessed neighbors' children, young men and women just out of high school, some recently married, some with new families, leaving Guyana and their children in the care of grandparents like my own parents had. I felt no bond with the kids who were left behind in Guyana like I was, except for the unmentioned sadness. A deep bond, though, was created with my older sister—the on-going separation from our parents pushed Dawn and I closer. We became one and the same; agreed it was best to stay mute around Adda to stay out of trouble. We no longer had to speak to each other to know what we were thinking and feeling. Gestures and codes became our form of communication.

Nothing much changed on Adda's end.

Oliver was school age and it was becoming clearer that he was not developing normally. In a blink, he would sneak out the school yard and find his way back to Granny's or sometimes Adda's house. Adda would look out the window to see him standing in the trench below. The drainage system long ago implemented was needed to collect rainfall that cokers dumped into the Atlantic Ocean. Otherwise, the citizens of our low-lying country would drown.

Oliver sat in the mucky waters in his school uniform all day and despite all the entreaties, coaxing, and threats from Adda made his way indoors only when darkness fell.

Oliver was drowning. Dawn tried her best to set the right example and follow the rules; it was the curse of the oldest sibling. I had not unraveled completely like Oliver, but I too was sinking.

In those days, a telephone call to the US was too expensive. Email and the internet didn't exist. The only way to contact my parents was to put pen to paper.

Dear Daddy and Mammy,
I feel unlucky.
I hate school. I cheat on tests and copy the correct answers from Dawn's old math and comprehension workbooks.
Adda is old-fashioned and doesn't allow us to go anywhere. I'm not her favorite grandchild. I know because she doesn't treat me like I'm her favorite. I want to run away and never go back to Adda's house. Why are the visas taking so long? I'm almost 12 and you're still not back. I'm wondering if the best thing is to forget about ever seeing you again. Maybe that would help.

Your daughter,
Ingrid

Of course, this letter was never sent.

PART III

TRANSITIONS

What we were in that other life, is shattered open. But the worlds
we now inhabit still speak of the need for invention, of ancestors, of faith.
In a time of literally explosive possibilities, we must figure out how to
live our lives.

Meena Alexander, *The Shock of Arrival*[1]

In *Transitions*, Grace Nichols (United Kingdom), Suchitra Mattai (United States), Christie Neptune (United States), and Sandra Brewster (Canada) reflect on how Guyanese women unfold a life in a past land to construct a new life in a new land. In these essays, poet Nichols and visual artists Mattai, Neptune, and Brewster detail the transition from citizen to immigrant. As the essays' titles suggest, each of their narratives has the acts of making and fashioning at their core—revision, weaving, embroidering, transferring, tracing. The women written about in *Transitions* struggle hard to get to their new lands, to be there, to belong, and to stay. We hear of Guyanese women who took on jobs and identities that required them to put themselves aside to be in service to others—other people's families, other people's homes, other people's empires. And, other people's dreams. In these essays, we witness how, through migration, Guyanese women are made, unmade, and remade again.

The space between departure and arrival is a terribly fragile one. As **Grace Nichols** pinpoints her first flight—her precise moment of leaving Guyana—she unravels how that singular moment of departure changed the course of her life forever. Her essay, 'So I Pick Up Me New-World-Self,' punctuated with poems ignited by her early years after her arrival in England, details the days when she embarked on the work of inventing the woman and writer she hoped to become. Within both her poems and her reflections, is a similar refrain for women who migrate: our acts of leaving are rarely, if ever, about desire. Instead, they are acts of necessity. Nichols likens her departure to a kind of rupturing, a severing. And then she is confronted with the shock of arrival and the stain of unbelonging thrust on her. As a Guyanese-born woman who has now lived in the United Kingdom longer than she has lived in her homeland, Nichols charts how we leave our old-world self to fashion, in her words, our 'new-world self.'

Throughout her oeuvre, artist **Suchitra Mattai** artistically reimagines and disrupts idealized landscapes. Her migratory path through three countries, Guyana, Canada,

    https://doi.org/10.11647/OBP.0218.10

and the United States, informs her artistic practice, characterized by what she deems 'disconnected "landscapes" that are unreal but offer a lingering familiarity.' In the selection of work featured in her art essay, 'Revisionist,' Mattai uses landscapes as both a symbolic device and a canvas to illustrate the liminal space of disorientation when one transitions through multiple cultural spheres. Mattai invokes a migration story started long before she left Guyana—that of her Indian ancestors brought by the British from India to the Caribbean, beginning in the 1830s and throughout the early 1900s, to work as indentured servants on British Guiana's sugar cane plantations. Mattai's landscapes, used to explore her relationship to the idea of homelands in transition, teem with texture, materiality, and laborious detail. To make this work, Mattai utilizes a bounty of objects and processes that are hand-done. They are a nod to the Guyanese women in her family who are experts in crocheting, weaving, embroidering, needlepointing, and sewing. With each puncture of embroidery, each woven thread, Mattai centers Indian women and the essential role they have played in three centuries of migration movements in and out of Guyana.

In her art essay, 'Memories from Yonder,' American-born artist **Christie Neptune** mines childhood memories of her mother, a Guyanese immigrant in New York, and her love of crocheting—a craft popular among Guyanese women (as we also see in Mattai's essay) and passed down through generations. For Neptune, the art of crocheting becomes a metaphor for the necessary acts of unfurling a life in a past land to construct a new life in a new land. Neptune unpacks her artistic process in making her multi-media installation. She portrays Ebora Calder, a fellow Guyanese immigrant and elder. Like the artist's mother, Ebora migrated to New York in the late 1950s and represents a generation of Guyanese women who in the past sixty years have been part of the mass migration from Guyana to New York City. In the installation, Neptune features a diptych of Ebora that has been distorted and obscured as well as a pixelated short video. In both photograph and video, Calder can be seen quietly engrossed in the slow, methodical, rhythmic act of crocheting a red bundle of yarn. 'The gesture serves as a symbolic weaving of the two cultural spheres,' writes Neptune, 'to reconcile the surmounting pressures of maintaining tradition whilst immersed in an Americanized culture.'

In 'A Trace | Evidence of Time Past,' Canadian-born artist **Sandra Brewster** elevates the voices of the matriarchs in her family. Brewster's family history of migration from Guyana beginning in the 1960s—a decade in which the country saw a tremendous exodus to Canada—parallels the emergence of Toronto as a prominent node in the Caribbean diaspora and one of the largest and oldest Guyanese populations outside of Guyana. As a daughter of immigrant parents, Brewster grew up hearing her family's stories of life in Georgetown—stories that simultaneously gave her a connection to Guyana as well as left her with questions. In her art essay, she generously mines those questions and offers us the stories, memories, and language of her grandmother,

mother, sister, aunts, and cousins whose words simultaneously trace a rupture and chart a chronology: What did it take to leave a beloved Guyana and build a life in an uncertain Canada? As Brewster documents that process, what is revealed is that it takes generations, it takes a whole family, it takes the driving force of women to get to a place of not merely surviving and adapting, but thriving.

The essays in *Transitions* implore us to ponder: How do we hold steadfast to our dreams, when in order to survive we must diminish parts of the self? As Nichols, Mattai, Brewster, and Neptune continue to center Guyanese women in their poetic and visual art practices, they reaffirm their laudable commitment to using their artistic practice as spaces for women of the Guyanese diaspora to speak, to be heard, and to be seen.

Notes

1. Epigraph from Meena Alexander, *The Shock of Arrival* (Boston: South End Press, 1996), p. 1. Used by courtesy of David Lelyveld.

8.

So I Pick Up Me New-World-Self

—

Grace Nichols

Figure 8.1

Grace Nichols with her daughter Lesley in Sussex, England in 1978—a year after her family migrated from Guyana. Grace Nichols Family Collection.

It was a cold morning on 3 November 1977 when I arrived in England with my partner John Agard and my four-year-old daughter, Lesley. We made our own way from London's Heathrow airport by underground to North London where John's dad lived. I remember shivering in my stylish but light pantsuit on that frosty autumn morning. Learning to dress in layers, in what the English call 'sensible clothes,' was a skill I'd take a while to acquire.

We were looking forward to being with John's dad who had migrated from Guyana and had been settled in England for a number of years. We came with the hope of becoming professional writers. John and I had met as young journalists working for one of Guyana's national newspapers, *The Chronicle*. John had a slim volume of self-published poems before we left Guyana, and I'd already written about half of my first and only novel, *Whole of a Morning Sky*. Apart from a government-owned press, there were no publishing houses in Guyana.

Coming to England was a big adventure—one that I hadn't even thought through. I was unprepared for how much I would miss home. Accustomed to seeing my sisters and brother nearly every day as well as other relatives and friends, England seemed the antithesis of this. Dropping around spontaneously to someone's home was not advisable. I soon learned to change my 'calypso ways.' Perhaps it was this emotional separation from Guyana that made me turn more and more to poetry, which was a deep love from childhood when I would dip into my father's poetry books.

Inspiration comes from all around, and of course, as a poet, you flow where the inspiration takes you. My collection, *The Insomnia Poems*, is a more personal work, an attempt to explore my inner landscape, which has been informed by my migration from Guyana to England, and the creative dynamics of being open to both my Caribbean and British heritages.

Now that I've lived in England for longer than I've lived in Guyana, I find that my sense of identity, my new-world-self, has grown more fluid. My 'Guyana-eye' still filters my experiences, but I'm also inspired by the chalk cliffs and rolling downs of Sussex where I've been living with my family for over thirty-five years and which I feel very close to.

How do you deal with living in another landscape when the older native one is so imprinted in your mind?

Going to see friends and relatives off at the airport was a regular feature of life in Guyana. When I was growing up in Georgetown, I often witnessed people leaving to 'better themselves' in North America and England. The 'Old Cane-Cutter at Airport' poem was inspired by an actual event—an elderly Indian man seeing his grandson off at the airport and witnessing the pain of parting, which we've come to accept as a natural part of our Caribbean experience but one that has a profound effect both on those leaving and the ones left behind.

Old Cane-Cutter at Airport

Boy going to join his mother in Canada,
study bad, turn lawyer.
Girl taking the flower of herself elsewhere,
turn nurse, maybe doctor.
Whole families sucked abroad.

Through the glass of the departure lounge
old cane-cutter watches it all—
face a study of diasporic brooding.
Watches the silver shark
waiting on the tarmac.

Watches until the shuddering monster
takes off with his one
and only grandson—
leaving behind a gaping hole
in the glittering sea we call sky.

But now, outside the airport building
where emotions are no longer checked in,
the old man surrenders to gut-instinct,
sinking to his knees on the grass.

His cane-shoot eyes
his voice cracked as he wails
what his bones know for certain;
'Nevaar to meet again
Nevaar to meet again.'

Come, Hanuman,
only your many arms
can help console this man—
still waving to an empty sky
the white flag of his handkerchief.

Grace Nichols, 'Old Cane-Cutter at Airport,' in *Startling the Flying Fish* (London: Virago, 2006), p. 56. © 2006 by Grace Nichols. Reprinted with the permission of the author.

'Wherever I Hang' was written shortly after coming to England in 1977. In those days, we were always being asked when we were going back home or if we intended to stay. The poem is a fairly light-hearted, tongue-in-cheek response to migration, but it hints at that feeling of 'unbelonging,' which we can all experience at times, even when we're living within our own culture. The title of the poem echoes the song from my teenage years: 'Wherever I Hang My Hat' by Sam Cooke.

Wherever I Hang

I leave me people, me land, me home,
For reasons, I not too sure
I forsake de sun
And de humming-bird splendour
Had big rats in de floorboard
So I pick up me new-world-self
And come to this place called England
At first, I feeling like I in dream
De misty greyness
I touching de walls to see if they real—
They solid to the seam
And de people pouring from de underground system
Like beans
And when I look up to de sky
I see Lord Nelson high—too high to lie

And is so I sending home photos of myself
Among de pigeons and de snow
And is so I warding off de cold
And is so, little by little
I begin to change my calypso ways—
Never visiting nobody
Before giving them clear warning
And waiting me turn in queue—
Now, after all this time
I get accustomed to de English life
But I still miss back-home side
To tell you de truth
I don't know really where I belaang

Yes, divided to de ocean
Divided to de bone

Wherever I hang me knickers—that's my home.

Grace Nichols, 'Wherever I Hang,' in *Lazy Thoughts of A Lazy Woman* (London: Virago, 1989), p. 10. © 1989 by Grace Nichols. Reprinted with the permission of the author.

A sense of place has always been important to me as a writer. Coming from Guyana—with its Atlantic coastline, its deep interior spirit of rivers, waterfalls, and vast rainforests—has made me into the kind of writer I am; one that keeps an eye on landscape and likes the elements to move in my work. But how do you deal with living in another landscape when the older native one is so imprinted in your mind?

I have been living in the south of England for many years now and that landscape, of rolling hills and chalky cliffs, is also a part of me. In 1987, England experienced a great storm of hurricane force and thousands of trees were uprooted where I lived. It had a big impact on my psyche. It was as if the old Gods from the Caribbean and Africa were in the winds around Sussex.

'Hurricane Hits England' remains a bridging poem between the two cultures.

Hurricane Hits England

It took a hurricane, to bring her closer
to the landscape.
Half the night she lay awake,
the howling ship of the wind,
its gathering rage,
like some dark ancestral spectre,
fearful and reassuring:

Talk to me Huracan
Talk to me Oya
Talk to me Shango
and Hattie
my sweeping back-home cousin.

Tell me why you visit
an English coast?
What is the meaning
of old tongues
reaping havoc in new places?

The blinding illumination
even as you short-
circuit us
into further darkness?

What is the meaning of trees
falling heavy as whales—
their crusted roots
their cratered graves?
O why is my heart unchained?

Tropical Oya of the weather,
I am aligning myself to you.
I am following the movement of your winds
I am riding the mystery of your storm.

Ah, sweet mystery,
come to break the frozen lake in me,
shaking the foundations of the very trees
within me.
Come to let me know—
That the earth is the earth is the earth.

Grace Nichols, 'Hurricane Hits England,' in *Sunris* (London: Virago, 1996), p. 34. © 1996 by Grace Nichols. Reprinted with the permission of the author.

To be in India is to feel both insignificant as an individual and yet part of the great universal heartbeat of life. The poem, 'Advice on Crossing a Street in Delhi,' was written after a visit to New Delhi in 2006, where John and I were invited to be part of a panel of judges for the Indian National Poetry Competition. India, like Africa, is one of the motherlands, so to speak, of the Caribbean, and I was struck by how certain aspects of life there mirrored my own childhood in Guyana. The jhandi flags fluttering on bamboo poles in front yards; sugarcane pressed into cane juice at roadside stalls; channa (chickpeas) parched and wrapped into little brown paper cones.

Advice on Crossing a Street in Delhi

First take a few moments to observe
the traffic's wayward symmetry.

While contemplating wheels of mortality,
note how whole families
on motorbikes dart daring
within the shifting shoal
of the cacophonous river.

Surely if they can, you too can
weave a quick trajectory.
So go—
at the first signs of a small break
with a great faith and a great surrender.

If stranded in the middle of the road
become a sacred cow with gilded horns
adopting the inner stillness of the lotus posture.
Let honking cars, rickshaws, lorries,
swarm or fly around you.

You are in the hands of the great mother.
The thing about India maybe
is to get the rhythm right—
this rhythm that will change the way
you cross a street forever.

Grace Nichols, 'Advice on Crossing a Street in Delhi' in *Picasso, I Want My Face Back* (Hexam: Bloodaxe Books, 2009), p. 47. © 2009 by Grace Nichols. Reprinted with the permission of the author.

9.

Revisionist

—

Suchitra Mattai

I left Guyana in 1977 when I was three years old, but Guyana has never left me. Through family narratives, memories, and photographs, I have always been reminded of my homeland, yet simultaneously felt alienated from it. My family's migratory path from Guyana to Canada to the United States never led to a place of connection. I have always felt 'othered' in so many ways. As a result, my life has been directed by a continual search for an imagined 'home.'

Making our journey first to Nova Scotia, Canada and eventually to various areas of the United States, I patiently waited to find a place that felt 'right.' In my twenties, I traveled to India, my original 'homeland.' On my first flight there, I looked through the window as the plane landed in New Delhi and was overcome with an inexplicable familiarity. But as I traveled throughout India, unable to communicate with ease, I quickly realized that this was not the 'right' place either. I would have to continue to look elsewhere.

My family, who first came as Indian indentured servants to British Guiana, is part of a history of ocean voyages to foreign lands by means of contracts of bondage. And so, as an artist, much of my practice is driven by this idea of an invented, idealized 'homeland.' My artwork is characterized by disconnected 'landscapes' that are unreal but offer a lingering familiarity. These landscapes are created from history, memory, travel, and pop culture. Many of the objects I use in my practice—embroidery, vintage needlepoints, macramé works, jewelry boxes, found photographs, teacups, and works on paper—are handmade, craft-based or domestic in nature. They are a nod to my Guyanese grandmothers, aunties, and mother, who engaged in practices of embroidery, macramé, crochet, and sewing during my childhood.

Thus, my work loosely weaves together a sense of an imagined 'home.' Through each puncture of embroidery, each woven thread, and each painted stroke, I am both bounded by and freed from my past, present, and future 'homes.'

    https://doi.org/10.11647/OBP.0218.12

Figure 9.1
Suchitra Mattai, 'Indentured' *(detail)*

2016, ribbon, rope and string on vintage macrame, artificial plants, graphite, acrylic, watercolor. Photo by Wes Magyar.

Indentured explores the continuity of generations through varied passages, including the passage of my ancestors from India to Guyana. The breaks and continuities in the 'landscape' communicate both the strengths and weaknesses of those bonds. The macramé piece that I 'appropriate' is 'colonized' in a way, becoming part of a larger narrative, much like the indentured laborers of Guyana. The handmade macramé references my childhood and my grandmothers' labor.

Figure 9.2
Suchitra Mattai, 'Indentured II'

2016, vintage chair, thread. Photo by Wes Magyar.

In *Indentured II*, I reconsider the power of colonialists and re-examine historical consequences. The chair—with its European design, aristocratic reference, and idyllic pastoral scenes in the fabric—is rendered useless. Its function is removed, and the historical power relations are subverted and thrown off-kilter. The thread that captures it references the domestic practices of my grandmothers, aunts, and mother.

Figure 9.3
Suchitra Mattai, 'Promised Land'
2016, video projection on furniture fragment. Photo by Wes Magyar.

I had the opportunity to travel on a ship across the Atlantic Ocean, retracing many of the steps of my Indian family, traversing the ocean for a better 'home.' The video in *Promised Land* is shaky and uncomfortable, forcing the viewer to experience the close quarters of the indentured laborers and the overwhelming nature of the vast unknown, as seen through the portal. The video is projected onto a furniture fragment, referencing the domestic.

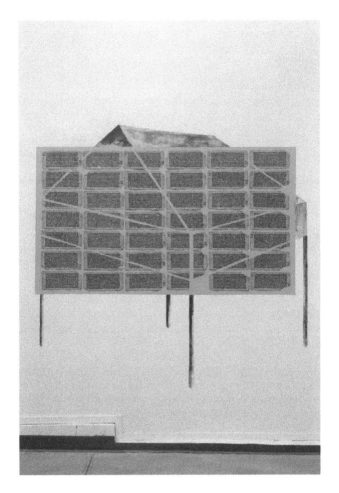

Figure 9.4
Suchitra Mattai, 'Homeward Unbound'
2016, Sanskrit text, acrylic paint, graphite. Photo by Wes Magyar.

The 'home' in *Homeward Unbound* is built of 'bricks' of old Sanskrit texts. The text holds religious power but is unreadable to the majority of Hindus in the world. I am interested in the fog of memory, how the past is shaped, built and transformed. The house in this piece references the homes on stilts in Guyana I grew up around.

Figure 9.5
Suchitra Mattai, 'Misfit'

2016, bindis on vintage painting. Photo by Wes Magyar.

I seek to hold onto a past that is sometimes intangible but always complex. In *Misfit* I take over an idealized European scene, though reminiscent of Guyana's Kaiteur Falls, with bindis. The bindis, a decorative mark worn in the middle of the forehead by Hindu women, reference the women of my family. Reserved for special occasions, the bindi was another nod to our past.

10.

Memories from Yonder

—

Christie Neptune

As a little girl, I spent my Saturday afternoons watching my mother, a Guyanese immigrant, crochet hats, scarves, and blankets for my brother, sister, and me. Her fingers would move rhythmically through interlocked loops of colorful yarn amidst the hums and chatter of daytime television. There was an elegance to her poise and movement.

With her legs crossed and a perfect posture, she moved autonomously, crocheting copious plains of complexed patterns with hook and yarn. After finishing one piece, she would quickly begin another. A huge yawn would bellow out from her after long stretches of time, followed by subtle twists and shifts until she found her next position.

My mother reminds me of the female genus Argiope: a precocious spider who constructs intricate stabilimentum (silk geometric structures) within the webbing of her orb. Although one might argue the functionality of the Argiope's labyrinth of webs, it is a rather conspicuous beauty to lay eyes on. Woven into its ornate structure lies a manifold of stories, mystery, and wonder; and like the genus Argiope, my mother's crocheted masterpieces beguiled me.

The art of crocheting is a popular recreational activity amongst Guyanese women. The act serves as a prophetic mode of maintaining home and family. On the eve of new life, the women crocheted blankets for the burgeoning mother; pillows and table runners for wives to be; and hats, scarves, and socks for the winter. For most, crocheting is a way of life; an intergenerational activity woven into a myriad of traditions. My great grandmother taught the art of crocheting to her daughters; and my grandmother taught it to my mother. Although I am an avid fan of the process, it is a talent I did not inherit.

In unspoken dialogues between my mother and myself, Saturday afternoons spent crocheting illuminated the transformative nature of identity. What does the economics of homemaking mean to a first generation American?

   https://doi.org/10.11647/OBP.0218.13

Never mixed with friends. No Husband. No Children.
But, I took care of children.

Figure 10.1
Christie Neptune, 'Memories from Yonder'
2015, diptych of archival inkjet prints.

I had a hard time adapting to this culture.

Figure 10.2
Christie Neptune, 'Memories from Yonder'
2015, diptych of archival inkjet prints.

In 2015, in an effort to reconcile my Guyanese heritage with my identity as an American, I interviewed elderly female immigrant seniors. During the course of six weeks, I collected personal reflections, life changing experiences, folklores, dreams and recollections that explored the socio-political constructs of identity, ethnicity and self. I asked, what happens when one's cultural foundations and values have shifted entirely because of a cultural landscape?

The result of the project was *Memories from Yonder*, an installation incorporating distorted photography and video, where I digitally weave together the visual narratives of Ebora Calder, a Guyanese immigrant and elder, my mother, and myself, a first-generation Guyanese-American artist. Calder's recollections set off a memory tape of childhood experiences, which explored the socio-politics of 'self' and identity. In her, I saw my mother and generations prior.

Calder (b. 1925, Georgetown, Guyana) migrated to America, in the late 1950s, in pursuit of the American dream. She worked in homecare before retiring in the Brooklyn Gardens Senior Center. To Calder, America was a 'strange' unruly place, which held neither peace, nor order. Her fondest memory in America was crocheting by the window while watching the snow fall. Like my mother, Calder crocheted multiple hats, scarves, and sweaters for children she provided care for.

In *Memories from Yonder*, Calder is depicted crocheting a red bundle of yarn. The gesture serves as a symbolic weaving of the two cultural spheres in an effort to reconcile the surmounting pressures of maintaining tradition whilst immersed in an Americanized culture. Like the Argiope's geometric constructions, *Memories from Yonder*'s digitally stitched manipulations explore the functionality and aesthetics of a new form.

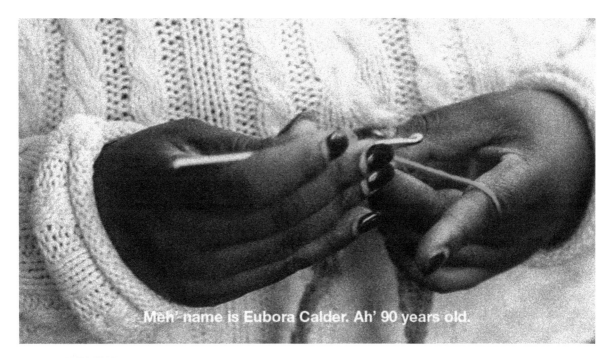

Figure 10.3
Christie Neptune, video stills from 'Memories from Yonder'
2015, video, 4 mins.

Figure 10.4

Installation view of Christie Neptune's 'Memories from Yonder', Photo by Argenis Apolinario. *Liminal Space'*, curated by Grace Aneiza Ali, Caribbean Cultural Center African Diaspora Institute (New York, NY), 17 June 2017–30 November 2017.

11.

A Trace | Evidence of Time Past

—

Sandra Brewster

Figure 11.1
Sandra Brewster, 'We Gather' (animation still)

included in 'A Trace | Evidence of Time Past', 2016–2017, charcoal on paper.

© Sandra Brewster. Courtesy of the artist. CC BY-NC-ND.

 https://doi.org/10.11647/OBP.0218.14

Figure 11.2

The Bullen family in Guyana, 1963. Brewster Family Collection.

Figure 11.3

My mother Carmen Brewster (then Bullen) arrived in Canada in December 1968. Brewster Family Collection.

The following essay is adapted from A Trace | Evidence of Time Past, *my 2017 thesis for the Master of Visual Studies degree at the University of Toronto. I examine the move of my family from Guyana to Toronto, through an expansion, in part, of techniques that I have been developing over time as an artist working with the photograph. The process of producing photographs using gel transfer is a time-consuming and laborious one. The pushing and pulling, rubbing and buffing assists in the removal of a covering layer of paper to reveal an image that now consists of creases, folds, and an emptiness where ink did not adhere. This process comprises a movement from one place to another place, an image that goes through a change. This change expresses a passage of time and offers a suggestion of untold stories and a deeper investigation into people and their experiences.*

A Trace *is grounded within the context of transfer: A move from one place to another. Relying on my memory and the memories of my parents, aunts, uncles, and my grandmother, I attempt to trace their journey from Guyana to Toronto and reflect upon the impact of this move on them and subsequent generations. Their stories have influenced the way I've formed a relationship with home, and sometimes have given me reasons as to why my home, here in Canada, doesn't always feel like home.*

My family's move to Canada interests me. Their decision shaped the rest of all of our lives, forever. Some shared stories, in the form of anecdotes, reflect their transfer from one place to another, and articulate how the shifts, switches, pushes, and pulls created adjustments to their identity. I suspect they leave an impression wherever they go, imprinting themselves in spaces of work, in hallways of high schools and universities, and on the stool of the bar they frequented one night a week. They also form Canadian organizations that bring Guyanese people together in order to embed their presence even further in the country. And when they have children, it is us who carry on their Guyanese ways no matter how diluted or fractured they may be.

*

Auntie Elo, the eldest, left Guyana first to find a place for everyone to live and to figure out the lay of the land so that when the others came, she could direct them on what to do and where to do it. She was their orientation guide to Canada.

This was the 1960s in the midst of the great influx of immigrants into the country. Guyana was not doing well economically, so my family took advantage of this opportunity to leave, despite how much they loved their country and their memories of how beautiful and thriving it once was. Over a period of time they organized themselves and headed north, hoping for a better quality of life for themselves and for anyone else who they imagined may come after.

My mother had always wanted to be a journalist. She has shared this with me and my sister many times. My Aunt Elo acted in the Theatre Guild in Guyana along with other members of the family. In my opinion, my father had the potential of being a really great draftsman. His desk-sized pad of graph paper was always covered with sketches of basement and bar designs and the occasional random drawing.

Sacrifices may have been made in order for these folks to establish themselves here—making choices that diverge away from their own true interests.

*

I asked Mom to report on the movement of the family from Guyana:

Gloria (who we call Elo), the oldest of the nine children born to Albert and Adelaide Bullen, left Guyana and settled in Toronto, Canada.

Conrad, the second oldest, joined the British Army while the Army was based in Georgetown Guyana on a peacekeeping assignment. After he joined the forces he was based in Germany and wherever the army sent him. I think it was in the Falkland Islands where he shot himself while cleaning his weapon. This injury damaged one of his lungs and he had that removed. He left the army and worked until retirement at Electric Company in London. He and his wife Denise lived in Kent, England, for several years then retired to Barbados, West Indies.

The third and fourth oldest left Guyana in 1967 and settled in Toronto, Canada. They went to live with the oldest, Gloria, at Ava Manor located at Bathurst and Eglinton.

On a bitterly cold, wintery night in December 1968, Joy and Carmen arrived and went to live at Ava Manor with Gloria, Una, and Raymond. The apartment was a two-bedroom at $159.00 per month.

Gloria, Raymond, and Una had jobs, so Gloria took Joy and Carmen to the Employment and Immigration Department the morning after arrival for them to apply for work.

Our father had passed away in 1968 and Mom was left in Guyana with the three youngest children, Sharon, Stephen, and Pauline.

Mom and the three arrived in March 1969 and we all moved to a three-bedroom townhouse (newly built) at Bathurst and Steeles. Soon a couple of friends moved in. Mom was in the habit of taking in friends who were new to Canada or had no family in Canada. There was always a full house, not unlike the way we lived in Guyana.

Una was engaged to Lennox Valladares. Lennox came to Canada on Una's sponsorship in early 1970 and they were soon married and moved to Gamble Avenue in the city. They later moved to Lawrence Avenue and Keele Street then to Burlington.

Leyland Brewster arrived in Canada on Carmen's sponsorship in May 1970 and they were married in August 1970. They stayed with the family at Bathurst Street and Steeles Avenue, later moving to Keele Street then Wilson Avenue, where the first child Sandra was born, then to Shaughnessy Boulevard, where Deborah was born. They moved once more, then to Malvern. When the children were nine and seven the family moved to Pickering, Ontario.

Maxey Bullen, a first cousin, and his fiancée Myrna Ogle came in 1969 and married that year. They lived in the city.

Eventually, one by one, siblings started moving out and my Gran moved to a new apartment in the Don Mills area. She made a living babysitting and eventually went to Burlington to live with Aunt Una, Uncle Lennox, and my two cousins, Tanya and Dion. And life just kept moving forward. Others would get married and the family continued to grow.

*

Whenever I ask an older person from the Caribbean—who came here during that same period of the late 1960s or early 1970s—to describe some of their first experiences in Canada, they often tell a variation of one story. Almost every time, someone shares their feelings upon seeing another person who 'looks like them.'

Unlike my family, many people came on their own, knowing only one or a few others. So, of course there was this urgent need to make new friends.

Depending on who I talk to, the scenario varies: walking down a street, grocery shopping, in the hallways of a new job. They all expressed an urgent need to perform some grand gesture like jumping the railing and risking a fall as they lunge downward towards the stranger to find out.

Where are you from?
When did you arrive?
Where do you live?
Where do you work?
Where are you going now?

*

I imagine my mom and dad, aunts and uncles, my grandmother—their bodies one by one and in various clusters at various intervals descending the steps of the plane . . . slightly shivering.

I wonder . . . How did the cold air feel on your cheeks? Flying in for that landing at Toronto International Airport—what did you think of the view from above?

And did you know what your next step would be?

My head is full of fractured memories formed from the stories told to me.

I can vividly share tales of Jeff, the family dog, chasing Uncle Maxey up the side of the house on East Street as he attempted to enter through the window past curfew. I remember Aunt Una protecting my mother by beating up school bullies after class then pushing them into the trenches on the side of the road. I can hear Aunt Joy's long piercing scream that traveled throughout the school hall just before the Head Mistress slapped her with a ruler in the palm of her hand for misbehaving.

I can feel the cool breeze by the Seawall where young lovers meet to sit and steal kisses. And I remember my grandmother picking fights with my grandfather, then leaving for the country where she would stay with her family for days and return with bundles of food and clothes for all the children.

I can feel the danger of cycling over uneven dirt roads, I can see the sunsets of the tropics, I can hear the sounds of small creatures at night, I can taste sapodilla, mango, papaya, aurora.

Figure 11.4

Sandra Brewster, *Stabroek Market* from *Place in Reflection*, 2016, gel medium image transfer on wood panel.

© Sandra Brewster. Courtesy of the artist. CC BY-NC-ND.

Figure 11.5

Sandra Brewster, *Cathedral*, from *Place in Reflection*, 2016, gel medium image transfer on wood panel.

© Sandra Brewster. Courtesy of the artist. CC BY-NC-ND.

Mom makes the country sound like a place of great wonders of the world:

Kaieteur Falls is the tallest natural one drop in the world! Bourda Market has the best fruit! Stabroek Market the best vegetables!

Our wooden cathedral is the most beautiful and it is the tallest wooden cathedral in the world! Our Botanical Gardens was the most lush!

The interior is the Amazon Jungle, you know! Don't walk in alone, not even one foot. You will be lost forever! It is dense and home to wild and dangerous animals!

The Essequibo and Demerara—these rivers are expansive. They flow forever and the water is a unique shade of brown, stained from the leaves of the surrounding trees.

Talking over each other, often loud, standing up with arms outstretched, motioning to demonstrate an experience, performing a scene that occurred over forty years ago! Each trying, for the umpteenth time, to convince the other that their version of the memory is correct. Each trying to convince us that they are correct. However, I recognized that they were not only attempting to one up each other; they were teaching us about back home.

They want us to experience what they experienced by flying us there, on the backs of their words.

I know they believe that we've missed out on something unique and rich. Possibly as rich as the brown color of the Essequibo; as rich as the complexity of the forest full of exotic animals, insects, and vegetation.

*

I leaf through old photographs delicately. I am always careful not to fray the edges, crease and fold the corners, or fingerprint the surface. The ones in our family are securely arranged and gathered in photo albums, envelopes, and boxes and stashed away safely waiting for us to find them when moments of nostalgia arise.

Sharing these books with new visitors, friends, and family is always exciting—and, at times, embarrassing—as we flip through the pages, attempting to identify places and people at different stages of their life. The experience feels like tracing the past. On every turn of a page the spine whines and creeks, revealing its age.

As I continue to scrutinize each picture, my fondness grows for these little pieces of paper memories. They are precious. When I look at the adults depicted, younger than I am now, I stare at their faces, expressions, and stances. I am so curious about what they carried with them, and what they left behind.

Over the years I've selectively lifted old photographs from various family albums. In the pictures, young people are presented in the trendy styles of their day, wearing yellow ochre turtlenecks, baby blue bell bottoms and big afros, looking slim and fresh from the Caribbean. The pictures are, for the most part, happy—full of joy and contentment. I can feel the excitement of a new adventure and a feeling of 'bring it on!' These pictures, taken not long after their arrival in Toronto from Guyana, convey an air of preparation with a 'what is next?' wonderment flowing through each scene.

Each picture is followed by an ellipsis.

And this is what inspires me. The pictures depict people who are not familiar with this new world that they've entered. With courage and intentionality, determined to move forward, they brought their full selves—what they left behind, who they are presently, and all the while looking forward to what is to come.

*

. . . we come full of ourselves—who we are and will become.[1]

Figure 11.6

Granny and my cousin Tanya, 1974. Brewster Family Collection.

My grandmother brought her full self here. I learned about the generous actions that she practiced in Guyana, then in Toronto. Granny welcomed family, friends, and strangers who ventured in and out of her home in Guyana. She encouraged a culture of hospitality, sharing, and generosity that continued during the early days in Toronto. People would pass through my grandmother's home for initial assistance from her or her children, their introduction to the city made easier.

Within the first few years of arriving in Toronto, over forty years ago, my mother and her friends started an organization that is now called The Seniors Guyanese Friendship Association. Wanting to facilitate a feeling of comfort within their parents, they created spaces and situations of active engagement for these senior Guyanese. New to the country and living in neighborhoods across Toronto, some did not even know that their good friends from back home were living in the same city! They reunited through weekly gatherings, brunches, dinners, dances, and excursions.

Over the years the seniors have traveled abroad and throughout Ontario, attending different events—plays at Stratford Festival, wine tasting in Niagara-on-the Lake and Prince Edward County. They experience the landscapes of places they would probably not have otherwise seen. They schedule meetings with city councilors to learn how to access services, police officers for safety tips, and health professionals for direction on good nutrition and exercise. Once a month they go bowling. And at the beginning of every Saturday meetup, they recite a prayer, then sing a song that wishes their community well. They also camp. Tug of War is the last game played before leaving the campgrounds after days of camaraderie. They pull and tug, using all of their strength, carefully, concluding their time together with this grand gesture.

*

The first Caribbean Festival in Toronto of 1967, that many still call Caribana (as it was previously known before its name changed due to corporate sponsorship), was also a gesture of generosity—a gift from the Caribbean community to Canada on its one hundredth birthday. I see this gift as an action that permanently transferred the community's existence onto the city, creating an undeniable presence in Canadian history.

Caribana invoked a strength of presence when thousands of people paraded along the streets of downtown Toronto. They first gathered at Varsity Stadium, then traveled east along Bloor Street, south on Yonge Street, turned right on Queen Street and completed the celebration in Nathan Phillips Square. This was where the backdrop of the then new City Hall became a symbol solidifying the presence of the Caribbean community. The people involved represent the same generation of people who are depicted in the collections of photographs I've compiled throughout the years.

My mom hustled us together and dressed us in comfortable, cool clothing; she made sure the laces of our running shoes were tied tight and our bellies full before heading out. It was the first weekend of August and like every year we were on our way downtown to celebrate in the streets for Caribana. For that entire Saturday afternoon on University Avenue people filled the width of the street from sidewalk to sidewalk. Loud calypso and soca erupted from gargantuan speakers of sound systems heavy on top of glitter-laden truck platforms elevated up high. Many of these trucks carried live bands backed up by dancers, followed by a troop of revelers. From above I'm sure we looked like a colony of a zillion ants bouncing up and down, all heading in the same direction.

The colors were intensely vibrant, the feathers from costumes wildly swayed back and forth so high they swept the bellies of clouds above. People wore masks twisted and contorted into exaggerated expressions, and large-scale wire sculptures jook-jooked upwards in rhythm to the sounds of the steel pan. We all moved together, we all moved south. The major streets had their own side movements—up . . . down . . . up . . . and down—as people entered and exited the College, Dundas, Osgoode, and St. Andrew subway stations. If they were not exiting or entering, they were simply looking for a roti or a dish of cook-up on the sides and corners of the streets—food necessary to keep up one's energy for the jump-up that was the parade.

At some point in between the greeting of family and friends, the nibbling of a patty, and Mom hollering at us to follow along, my sister and I would escape into the throngs of people following the bands. Each person was always situated very close to the next person, and while the bodies moved to the music, I felt mine rise. A slow, eventual ascent . . . upward. There were times when my feet were not even touching the ground! Amazed, I'd laugh and simply enjoy being carried away.

*

I like old photographs because of their tactile characteristics. The glossy surface, the cracks in the image and the borders around the pictures transfer a feeling of time. I can feel them before I pick them up. More recent photographs seemed to have become pristine and sharp—the nostalgic qualities found not only in the depictions but felt in the materiality of the photograph are gone.

I don't know anyone who prints photographs anymore. My mom tried to hold onto the practice. It took her a while to move on from her point-and-shoot film camera. 'It takes really good pictures,' she would insist again and again whenever we went on a trip. She still uses it at times although she has been getting used to the camera on her phone, convinced that it also takes really good pictures.

Markings from subtle creases, tears, folds, and bent corners are a result of their journey from hand to hand, box to box, house to house, and from page to page as bookmarks. I think that these qualities assist with a deeper reading of the content. The pictures become ghostly, depicting the essence of the people in the photograph, not only their form. The physical markings of these pictures have me reading beyond the surface. Rather than simply enjoying the recognition of who is in the picture and admiring the scene, I wonder about their past, present, and future. It is as though I'm reading a story within the frame.

Figure 11.7

Pauline, Sharon, and Gloria, posing on a hill in the Guyana interior (unknown year). Brewster Family Collection.

Figure 11.8

In the background is the work *Town Girls a Top the Hill*, based on the photograph above (Fig. 11.7). In the foreground on the left is *Heirloom*, my sister's jar of currents and fruits soaking in rum and wine in preparation for Black Cake. On the right, hanging from the ceiling are images of the Essequibo River transferred to mylar. *A Trace | Evidence of Time Past* (installation view), 2017. Art Museum, University of Toronto Art Centre, Master of Visual Studies, University of Toronto, Canada. Photo by Toni Hafkenscheid.

Figure 11.9

My sister Debbie (age three) and me (age five) in our house in Malvern, 1978. Brewster Family Collection.

Heirloom (Fig. 11.8) is a jar that contains the ingredients that are processing together, a form of transfer as well, to make Black Cake. Rum, wine, cherries, fruit, and currents soak for months; ingredients that have a complex history in and of themselves are still used to bring Caribbean communities together. This jar is my sister's jar (Fig. 11.9) and she is the baker of this cake. The cultural tradition has transferred down to her. I personally am unaware of anyone of my generation who makes Black Cake.

This makes the jar very special. Special in terms of its content and the importance that it brings to bonding communities and within the context of a contemporary exhibition it represents something that possibly only those who are acquainted with it would recognize. I see the jar as a symbol of presence.

*

No sitter needed. We would jump into the backseat of the Malibu and ride with our parents to their basement parties. Intentional or not, these nights taught us about community and the importance of sticking together. Everyone who attended was a member of our extended family.

We grew up with aunts, uncles, and cousins who are not found in our blood line. Some cousins were called aunts and uncles because they were much older. Uncle Maxey, for example, is a cousin, not an Uncle. But I couldn't imagine calling him 'Maxey.' And 'Cousin Maxey' just seems odd, and lacks the respect that Uncle suggests.

Aunt Sharon likes to collect family. She introduces us to random people at random events with an air of absolute surprise at the discovery of their presence. Her famous method of introduction is presenting us as the child of someone 'This is Carmen's daughter!' then, turning to me, 'Mandy, this is So and So. She is the sister of So and So, your second cousin, daughter of our Uncle So and So.' There are so many of these relatives introduced to us that I can't keep track of who is who. I seldom pay attention during the introduction or I duck and escape when I see one about to happen.

Aunt Sharon is excited by the vastness of our family, spread out across cities, provinces, and countries.

*

We stood along the busy shoreline. After some negotiating, making deals for how much and for how many, we climbed into a small blue and white speedboat. We were about to travel along the Essequibo River.

I was disobeying my mother. 'Don't go into that speed boat,' she said waving her finger at me as I headed to Pearson Airport for Georgetown, Guyana with Aunt Joy. My aunt was taking the trip to reunite with a friend and with home. Like most of her siblings, she hadn't been back for many years and invited me to join her.

After a trip to the Essequibo years ago, my mom returned with stories of feeling unsteady and unsafe in the boat. I understood as we were all tilted back in the tiny vessel. Mom probably felt that at any point, at any time, there may be a bump or a sharp unexpected turn that would cause her to topple over into the river. She did not want to consider the possibility of me falling in either.

The boat pulsated up and down as it sped along. The wind blew past and through us. We hung tight as the rapids grew stronger. The river is immense. At times, it was hard to take in, while teetering and tottering and struggling to steady myself. It was so loud that we were yelling at each other in order to be heard over the roar of the engine and the crash of the waves. Both at the same pitch.

I peered up and allowed my eyes to follow the flock of birds swirling together, forming an elegant 'S' again and again.

Eventually, we calmed as the river calmed, and, finally, sat in silence to experience the beauty and quiet of the Essequibo.

The color of the water has been described as café au lait. The water is stained by the tannins from the leaves that fall from the surrounding trees, the vegetation, rocks and other naturally occurring elements—sediment that travels from shore to the depths of the river. So much happens below the surface.

As we drifted in silence, our guide pointed towards a line in the river. He explained that the line divided two directions of flow. Each flow had a slightly different shade of brown. We traveled along one direction of flow, then crossed over to the other.

As we moved from one line to the other, the boat slightly shifted and eventually flowed in the same direction as the water beneath us. Tiny laps of waves hit our sides then quieted as we fell in line. Like the piranhas swimming alongside, waiting to nibble on my fingertips, and the birds flying in tandem above, we all moved from one place to the next place together.

Similar to a generation of people from the Caribbean who picked up and moved on to experience another life, an adventure that may have at times felt like a rush through rough waters.

Figure 11.10
Sandra Brewster, 'We Gather' (animation still)

included in 'A Trace | Evidence of Time Past', 2016–2017. Charcoal on paper.

Notes

1. Dionne Brand, *Bread Out of Stone: Recollections, Sex, Recognitions, Race, Dreaming and Politics* (Toronto: Coach House Books, 1998), p. 138.

PART IV

RETURNS, REUNIONS, AND RITUALS

The joy of coming back to a country I called home was always
punctuated by explaining why I deserved to call it home in the first place.

Rida Bilgrami, 'Why Do Borders and Passports Dictate
What Country I Get to Call Home'[1]

For those of us—in the millions[2]—who have left one country for another, how do we return? And after we do, how do we stay connected? What tangible things do we cling to? In Part IV, *Returns, Reunions, and Rituals*, Michelle Joan Wilkinson (United States), Maria del Pilar Kaladeen (United Kingdom), and Maya Mackrandilal (United States) do not rest solely on gazing back at a homeland from an outsider distance. Instead, each of their essays explore their returns to Guyana and the ways in which they choose to remain tethered to the houses, lands, and sacred heirlooms embedded within their family legacies. Connecting these three women—all of whom were born in the diaspora—is a deep desire to know the land of their parent's birth. In their returns, they have ended decades-long estrangements from Guyana, reunited with relatives they've known from a distance through telephone calls and letters, and created new rituals to honor the loved ones they never knew.

'What gets left when we migrate?' is the question American-born curator **Michelle Joan Wilkinson** poses as she opens her curatorial essay, 'Concrete and Filigree.' Within that initial question, we are left to ponder its subtext: What are the objects we choose to carry when we leave a place? How do we decide, when we leave a homeland, which of our possessions become worthy to migrate with us? Writing from a curatorial perspective, Wilkinson explores two deeply personal objects that engage this duality of what we leave and what we carry. Concrete and filigree function as inheritances that connect Wilkinson to her grandfather and grandmother, and, by extension, to Guyana. A concrete house built by her grandfather literally roots Wilkinson in Guyana's soil; and a treasure trove of gold filigree jewelry passed down to generations of Wilkinson women is a reminder of her family's traditions. While noting the tremendous responsibility of caring for the things we either inherit or carry with us from our homelands, Wilkinson's essay reminds us that in small and grand ways, we are all the caretakers of our family's stories.

  https://doi.org/10.11647/OBP.0218.15

Maria del Pilar Kaladeen opens her memoir-essay, 'A Daughter's Journey from Indenture to Windrush,' with the passport portrait page of her father Paul Kaladeen. The black and white portrait is stamped in 1961, the year Paul left British Guiana for the United Kingdom. He would return some forty-five years later with his daughter. The passport photo is a document of agency, of one's freedom, or lack thereof, to move about the world. The portrait of Kaladeen's father, taken in a moment of great transition for a young man, is full of possibility and promise. Yet, for many decades after his migration, there was silence about his homeland. Without a sense of her family's roots to ground her identity in, Kaladeen writes of the racism she endured growing up in the United Kingdom as a daughter of immigrants and the pressures, including from her parents, to shirk her cultural identity and be monolithically 'British.' It was Kaladeen's desire to know the land of her father's birth that served as the catalyst to end his four-decade estrangement from Guyana. Their intertwined story illustrates the fractures and fissures migration creates in relationships and simultaneously, the sheer willpower required to rebuild a bridge between two lands and between a father and daughter.

To create the body of work 'Keeping Wake' featured in her art essay, American-born artist **Maya Mackrandilal** journeyed to Guyana in 2011. She returned to the rice fields where her Guyanese-born mother grew up, until she too left as a young woman. We find Mackrandilal in the midst of loss and death as rituals and preparations are made for her grandmother's funeral. Water is a key symbol throughout 'Keeping Wake.' Mackrandilal paints vivid scenes that mirror the crossing of the *kal pani*—Hindi for 'dark waters'—conjuring the traumatic voyage of Indian indentured laborers from India to British Guiana. We are reminded that the history of the Indian crossing into Guyana is a dark one. Indeed, contributors Suchitra Mattai and Maria del Pilar Kaladeen also poignantly link their migration stories to their Indian family legacies. Between 1838 and 1917, over 500 ship voyages deposited more than a quarter-million men and women from India to British Guiana's Atlantic coast. They would spend over eight decades toiling on sugar plantations and rice fields. Mackrandilal connects generations of those who ventured into the *kal pani* two centuries ago with those who embark on symbolic crossings of their own twenty-first-century dark waters. The rupture created by the initial crossing of the *kal pani* remains pervasive. It now haunts a second wave of migration, this time from Guyana to the United States. As she contemplates the past, questioning why the majority of the indentured laborers never returned to India, Mackrandilal draws comparisons to the distance she and her mother now experience with Guyana and reflects on their absence in their homeland. She ponders an important question for us all in the poignant narration of her 2014 video work, *Kal/Pani*, 'Acres of rice farm in a country we rarely visit [...] what are we, the generation that exists in the wake of estrangement, to make of the pieces?'[3]

Collectively, the essays in *Returns, Reunions, and Rituals* explore how daughters of immigrants like Wilkinson, Kaladeen, and Mackrandilal have rekindled, restored, and repaired frayed bonds. For those in the diaspora still estranged from Guyana, they illuminate how to rediscover a place once lost.

Notes

1. Epigraph from Rida Bilgrami, 'Why Do Borders and Passports Dictate What Country I Get to Call Home,' *Catapult*, 19 September 2019, https://catapult.co/stories/becoming-british-uk-citizen-passports-borders-immigration-rida-bilgrami. Used by courtesy of Rida Bilgrami.

2. According to the United Nations' most recent study on global migration, 258 million people are now living in a country other than the one they were born in, marking an astonishing increase from 173 million people in 2000. Elisa Mosler Vidal and Jasper Dag Tjaden, *Global Migration Indicators 2018* (Berlin: Global Migration Data Analysis Centre (GMDAC) and United Nations International Organization for Migration, 2018), https://publications.iom.int/system/files/pdf/global_migration_indicators_2018.pdf

3. Maya Mackrandilal, *Kal/Pani*, 2014, SD video with sound, 8:53 mins, https://mayamackrandilal.com/section/417745-Kal-Pani.html. See also curatorial statement (pp. 62–65) in the exhibition catalogue for 'Un |Fixed Homeland' curated by Grace Aneiza Ali, at Aljira, a Center for Contemporary Art, (Newark, NJ), 17 July–23 September 2016, https://view.joomag.com/un-fixed-homeland-aljira-center-for-contemporary-art-2016-catalog-un-fixed-homeland/0430951001481910086?short

12.

Concrete and Filigree

—

Michelle Joan Wilkinson[1]

Lost and Found in Migration

Lost Words

Verandah
Public Road
Filigree
Sweeties
Granny

What gets left behind when we migrate? We lose not only the spaces our bodies once held; we lose also the words to name those spaces. Words like verandah. We make these words a language of their own, local and intimate, used when family is around because they will understand. If we write, we reclaim the lost words and put them on the page like a tally of belongings or to dos.

But memory is a rabbit hole, and once a picture appears in our mind's eye, once a word resounds in our ears, we begin to conceive again the time, the place, the feeling, the scene. We use the words we can remember to reinvent that moment. We marry imagination with nostalgia. But we also ask questions to those who were there. What do *you* remember? We write it down. We record them. We balance corroboration, illumination, exaggeration.

We arrange the View-Master in our minds and we rehearse the script in our heads. We search the home videos for clues. We create again a world which we believe we knew, hoping it passes the inspection of pointed fingers and wagging tongues. Hoping its truth is one we can all live with.

    https://doi.org/10.11647/OBP.0218.16

Figure 12.1

My grandmother, Miriam Angelina Wilkinson, and me visiting Brooklyn, New York in 1977. Personal collection of Michelle Joan Wilkinson.

We wonder, what will they say of this world on the page?

We ask, who will care for these relics, the lost words, and the forgotten things they describe?

We look inwards. What can we do?

Found Words

Curator
Archive
Poet
Collection
Museum

Curator n. one who curates. A person in charge of the things in a museum. Derived from the Latin *curare*, to care and to take care of.

I am a curator. By definition, I am 'responsible for the things.' I work at the intersections of memory and preservation, of caring for things that are or need to be remembered. I am not haunted by the past, nor do I feel a need to hoard it. But there is comfort in knowing where I came from.

There is joy in discovering the things that others have left, and pride in holding onto the things that have been left for me.

In my family, concrete and filigree have passed through generations. They are among my inheritances. One connects me to my grandfather, the other to my grandmother.

Beyond being a caretaker of things in a museum, a guardian of things in a collection, I want also to preserve what is passed down within my family, from grandparent to granddaughter, aunt to niece, mother to child. And I imagine, how will my time here be remembered—what things will I leave behind?

Leaving Home, Coming Back

I.

My mother migrated to Brooklyn, New York in 1969. She came with a reference letter from her employer in Guyana, which helped her secure a job in Manhattan's Garment District within days of her arrival. Several weeks later her older sister landed. As new immigrants, they found refuge in the Caribbean-American enclaves of Brooklyn, sharing a brownstone with other families. Grown women, in their thirties by the time they emigrated, their new lives were full-on adulting.

And then came me. I arrived one December evening in 1971. I had spent the last nine months swirling in embryonic fluid with my little playmate, my twin brother Michael. But days before our birth, something happened. We still don't know what. But he didn't make it out into this world. Stillborn. My playmate was gone.

Single and working a good job, my mom had some decisions to make about my future. If I stayed in Brooklyn, who would take care of me and how much would it cost? If I went to live with my grandmother in Guyana, who suggested my mother send me there, what kind of life would I have 'back home?' And though she wasn't married to my father, and though he didn't seem to know how to claim me, would sending me to Guyana be fair to him—a twenty-something Black American man who would likely never go to Guyana to visit this surprise of a daughter.

In early 1972, I went to live with my grandparents. I lived in a house my mother and her sister only knew as adults, a house they had helped build in their late teens and twenties. That house was where I grew up, where I learned my ABCs, to count, and to read. It is where I learned to express myself—to talk and to talk back. (Yes, they called me fresh.)

Mom would visit, and I would go to the States for holiday, accompanied by my grandmother. I knew I was American. I knew my mother was abroad. But I also knew that home was the house my grandfather built, where Granny and I shared a room, and Grandpappie's room was next door, and my Indian friends lived down the road. Sometimes I would go into town with Granny, but we'd always come back to the house on Public Road.

II.

In 1977, I started primary school in our local village, a dozen miles from Georgetown. Within weeks, my grandmother died. Everyone came home to take care of things. When those things were settled, I was back on a plane to start my new life in Brooklyn with my mother and aunt. I was five years old. I started elementary school as a first grader in September. I was the girl in the class with the accent. If I was American, I was differently so. But then again, this was Brooklyn in the late 1970s. There were kids whose parents where from Nigeria, Puerto Rico, Panama, Haiti, and like those kids, within weeks I spoke like a Brooklynite, not a girl from the place where her mother was born. I got busy being and becoming this new me.

In 1993, at age twenty-one, after living away from Guyana for almost fifteen years, I returned to see where I came from, so to speak. My grandfather had died in 1978, just a year after Granny, but some of our relatives still lived in the house I grew up in. When I entered the home, I was amazed at how small it seemed, its handsome contours made miniature as my adult body roamed its spaces. I was the one who had grown. It was no longer the playground it had been when I was a child, where every wall seemed to be a surface for drawing, where every corner seemed to hold trinkets for my amusement, where my grandparents indulged my whims and chatter. They were gone now. But as I began to bask in those memories, the house became big again, swelling with the pride of a place well-remembered.

Upon returning to the States, I couldn't stop thinking about my trip, my trajectory from South America to North America, what I had lost and what I had exchanged. I began to write. I wrote a poem titled 'Guyana Quintet,' taking inspiration from the critically-acclaimed Guyanese novelist Wilson Harris, who had published a series of four novels collectively referred to as *The Guyana Quartet*. Within my five-part prose poem, I titled one section 'V is for Veranda,' offering:

> In the house of my childhood, like any real house of childhood, there was a veranda. I remember when it was taller than me and when I grew past it. I could see outside then, onto the Public Road. And I could look down into our yard and see the trees—now barren, now blooming. On the veranda, I myself was Barbie before she came to me packaged and blond. I reigned in that dream house . . . I owned that space above the open porch and patio. Ver-an-dah. My autopilot eyes sailing across a sea of green palm leaves with yellow patches. My own dream house, full-sized and first class.

I didn't see any verandas in Brooklyn. I lost that word. Buried under new vocabulary, veranda muted to balcony. But all along I knew it; that it wasn't the same. Buildings had balconies, but a house, a house had a veranda.

In the poem, I am speaking to the loss of language as much as to the loss of space, and how these two are related. The language of my childhood gave visibility to spaces that no longer existed in my American life. By returning to Guyana, I was re-learning a lost vocabulary and re-connecting to a poetics of space that had shaped my first ideas of home.

Concrete Legacies: My Grandfather

Figure 12.2

Grandfather Charles Eric Wilkinson (unknown date). Personal collection of Michelle Joan Wilkinson.

Figure 12.3

View of house in East Coast Demerara, Guyana (unknown date). Personal collection of Michelle Joan Wilkinson.

What do families choose to keep, what do they pass on? My grandfather left my mother and my aunt a concrete house, each. Houses in another country. One of those houses is the one I grew up in.

The House that Grandfather Built

Charles Eric Wilkinson designed and built a concrete house in 1954 with the assistance of his family and others. Initially, a two-story wooden house stood on the land. Around 1951, he bought the wooden house with the intention of tearing it down to build a new concrete home for his family on the same land. As a building contractor, he had designed and constructed several concrete buildings for commercial clients, but this was the first concrete structure he purposely built as a residence. Wilkinson employed advanced engineering techniques to build the house. After excavating the site, he fortified the foundation by driving thirty-foot timbers into the ground, then he erected its steel-framed walls with poured concrete. From its timber pile foundation to its second-floor vistas, the home exemplified the most contemporary international ideas for architecture and construction in the mid-twentieth century.

Wilkinson's decision to construct the house of concrete was not only innovative but calculated. Guyana was experiencing a 'dark time,' as the Guyanese poet Martin Carter would deem the period in 1953, when armed British troops landed in its capital Georgetown seeking to disrupt the progress towards gaining independence led by the newly allied political parties of Afro-Guyanese and Indo-Guyanese changemakers. The British government feared the left-leaning alliance would threaten Britain's ability to maintain control of the colony. Blacks and Indians were pitted against each other, with some, like Carter, arrested for dissention. As Carter wrote in 'This is the Dark Time, My Love,'

> It is the season of oppression, dark metal, and tears.
> It is the festival of guns, the carnival of misery,

The poet cautioned his compatriots about the stealth movements of

> . . . the strange invader
> watching you sleep and aiming at your dream.[2]

I marvel at Grandfather Wilkinson's ability to erect a concrete house in the period that he did. In this climate of a colonial coup d'état, inter-ethnic antagonisms, and local agendas for independence, he seemingly endeavored to construct an indestructible oasis. Neighbors speculated on what he was building. Was it just a nice, respectable home for a family of some means, or a veritable fort that could not easily be shot at and destroyed?

The Verandah Diaries

I've long been intrigued by verandahs. They exist in that liminal space between inside and outside, publicity and intimacy, sight and oversight. But a verandah does not happen by chance; someone, in this case, Charles Eric Wilkinson, set out to design his first concrete house with a verandah. I know this, because I have the 1954 blueprint. I also have letters he wrote to my mother and aunt, many of them describing my early years in the house.

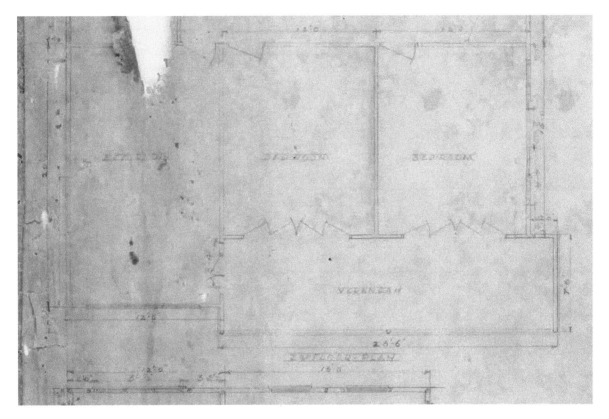

Figure 12.4

This ca. 1954 plan for the house shows the allocation of rooms, including a verandah on the second floor. Photo by Walter Larrimore/NMAAHC. Personal collection of Michelle Joan Wilkinson.

. . . I find her amusing every morning I take her to the verandah and she keeps enjoying herself with the different scenes, from cart to car to bus, to man to dog and every imaginable thing . . .

—Grandfather Wilkinson to my aunt, 10 June 1972

For a later concrete home he built, Wilkinson created a verandah with a metal railing. He used perforated walls on the ground floor to help circulate breeze through the spaces of the home. Were these differences seen as improvements upon the design of the first home he'd built, or were these specifications implemented per his clients' request? I don't know. But he did write a letter to my mother about how the government was building a new road and this house was in a path they sought to claim in 1972.

In the same letter that my grandfather recounts my escapades on the verandah, he also tells his daughter, my aunt, about his tribulations in getting an appraisal done for the land on which the family home sits. It's a tale of government run-arounds with the intent to extract money above and beyond what is entitled—not an unusual scenario. After taking up his issues with a higher-ranking official, Wilkinson reveals he was able to get a fair estimation on the amount of taxes to be paid for the land.

Sunday, I am hoping to start putting on some paint on the outside of the house at least trying to brighten for the 10th Independence anniversary . . .

—Grandfather Wilkinson to my mother, 10 April 1976

In his many letters to my mother and aunt, my grandfather would cover a range of subjects, from his work as a member of the Central Housing and Planning Authority, to who next was trying to get papers to go abroad, to politics and current events in Guyana, to (reluctantly asking for) what products and construction tools he needed sent from America, often signing off 'Cheerio, Dad.'

Filigree Heirlooms: My Grandmother

Figure 12.5

Grandmother Miriam Angelina Wilkinson (unknown date). Personal collection of Michelle Joan Wilkinson.

Granny's Filigrees

I've never shopped for filigree jewelry of my own. My grandmother did. When she died in 1977, she left me several pieces: chains, rings, filigree earrings, and bands. I was five then, and I couldn't wear them. I still don't. Granny was a full-grown woman when she died. Turban upright, back straight, shoulders down, arms solid. She wasn't a petite little thing like me, with my thin fingers and narrow wrist. Granny's filigrees would slip and slide on my arms, end up in somebody's lost-and-found. Filigree fanciness decorating someone else's life. No. I will wear them in my grave.

Mother: What did you say? Morbid. Please tell me you are joking.

Aunt: You better not plan on that. You want people to . . .

Child: I want to be bejeweled like the Egyptian goddesses, bedecked like a Queen Mother in gold and metals, returning them and me to the earth. I want to wear them where they can't fall off.

Mother and Aunt: [Suck teeth in unison]

The way my mother tells it is this:

Well, when your Granny died we saved most of her jewelry for you. I took a few things, your aunt took a few, and rest we put away for you. I wish you would wear them when you have your special events. I mean, what's the point in just keeping them packed away. They are meant to be worn. I could understand why you didn't wear them before, because yes you didn't want to lose them, but now, you should be wearing them. I hate that you say you want to be buried with it. Really? How morbid. You can't take it with you, you know. You want people to rob your grave? I don't get it. Wear it now.

Figure 12.6

Assortment of gold jewelry I inherited when Granny died in 1977. Photo by Walter Larrimore/NMAAHC.

Filigree Jewelry

Necklace, two pairs of 'chandelier-style' earrings, pin, and ring. Worn by Miriam Angelina Wilkinson. Designed and made by a local Indian jeweler, ca. 1960.

Gold 'Slave Band'

The 'Slave Band' was a popular style of jewelry in the 1950s and 1960s. Mother recalls that Elizabeth Taylor's portrayal of 'Cleopatra' spawned a craze for jewelry where people wanted the type of arm and wrist bands worn in the film.

Gold Bangles: History and Heritage

Much-coveted, long-cherished, ceremonially acquired, or proudly purchased, gold bangles enjoy an almost ritual status among Guyanese of all ages. But why? In the Guianas, gold has been the subject of lore historically associated with the mythic city of El Dorado that captivated the European explorers' pursuits. The arrival of Africans in the 1600s forged new legacies for gold in Guyana. The style of my grandmother's gold bangles is a remnant from 'manillas'—the brass and copper, horseshoe-shaped bracelets worn in West Africa. Manillas were originally worn to display wealth and later adopted as a form of currency, especially for purchasing enslaved Africans. Over time and across cultures, bangles acquired different meanings. Guyanese who wear bangles today may not be aware that similar bracelets had associations with slavery, but they may relate these valued items to one's social status or displays of material assets. More than an attractive accessory, gold bangles are symbolic links to a diasporic heritage. They honor Afro-Guyanese traditions of adornment and employ Indo-Guyanese practices of jewelry making, both of which have kept the style alive.

First Proof is Gold

Silver is for when you are older and taking the IRT by yourself.
First proof is gold circling baby wrists—clinging to the fat
and bone as tight as baby's fingers closing to a fist.

Gold like my grandmother's tooth.

Dull like the grays of her hair.

Shiny like her black wig.

A browning gold, like the Guyana waters rising against the sea wall.
Rising against the height of Persaud's Jewelry Palace,
just next to Sanji's Candy Shoppe,
where Granny buys us sweeties.
Sweeties that rot teeth early
and later turn them to gold.

Figure 12.7

'Michelle' name plate gold chain, ca. 1983. Photo by Walter Larrimore/NMAAHC.

Of Things Remembered

When I was younger and we would go to the mall in Brooklyn, my aunt always wanted to stop at 'Things Remembered,' a variety store where you could buy cards, stationery, photo frames, and get things engraved. It was such a strange place to me, especially in a shopping mall bustling with a movie theater, Orange Julius, Joyce Leslie, and an arcade. But what did I know, I was maybe ten.

At that age, I had a small but potent catalog of things remembered from Guyana: an afternoon flying kites with Grandpappie in the nearby pasture; singing along as 'Sandrowta,' my favorite chutney tune, churned on the record player; the smell of Limacol and Ben Gay accompanied by the billowing of lace curtains in Granny's room. Looking back now, I can better appreciate our visits to a store that helped people preserve their memories.

Today, my keepsakes include handwritten letters from grandparents, fading photographs, a blueprint for a house, and reels of jaunty Super 8 film my mother shot of my last day living in Guyana. But none of these items were left for me—they are what I took, or what I asked to have. Unlike concrete, unlike filigree, which purposefully passed between generations in my family, these other inheritances are those which I sought out and saved.

Being a guardian is an honor and a responsibility.

What does it mean to inherit?

For me, it is being a link in that chain with my name on it, reuniting things (almost) lost with things remembered.

This way of knowing and communing with one's past is part truth, part history, part regeneration. As African American poet Kevin Young has written, 'it is this reason I found myself a poet and a collector and now a curator: to save what we didn't even know needed saving.'[3] This is what I have found, as well. I've been a poet honing the moments of my own life, a collector amassing my family's stories, and now a curator caring for the heirlooms and archives that I share with you.

Notes

1.   'Concrete and Filigree' includes excerpts from material published in *ARC* magazine and the *International Review of African American Art*. See Michelle Joan Wilkinson, '"Guyana Quintet" and "Gold Bangles,"' *ARC Magazine: Contemporary Visual Art and Culture*, 3 (2011), 20–21. See Michelle Joan Wilkinson, 'Not Grandpa's Porch, Or Is It?: Musings on the New Museum on the Mall,' *International Review of African American Art*, 25/2 (2015), 52–61.

2.   Martin Carter, 'This is the Dark Time, My Love,' in *Poems of Resistance from British Guiana* (London: Lawrence and Wishart, 1954), p. 14.

3.   Kevin Young, *The Grey Album: On the Blackness of Blackness* (Minneapolis: Graywolf Press, 2012), p. 14.

13.

A Daughter's Journey
from Indenture to Windrush

—

Maria del Pilar Kaladeen

Figure 13.1

The passport page features the portrait of my father, Paul Kaladeen, who left Guyana (then British Guiana) in 1961. It would be forty-five years before he would see his country of birth again. Maria del Pilar Kaladeen Family Collection.

    https://doi.org/10.11647/OBP.0218.17

I grew up knowing nothing about the history or culture of my father. Courtesy of the British Empire, I am the by-product of two mass migrations: the migration of my great grandparents from India to Guyana in the latter part of the nineteenth century as Indian indentured laborers; and the migration of my father, Paul, from then British Guiana to the United Kingdom in 1961. Paul was part of what later became known in Britain as the 'Windrush Generation.'[1] The first of his four siblings to leave Guyana, he was also the only one who chose to come to the United Kingdom, while his siblings were part of a later migration to Canada. He left British Guiana's capital Georgetown by boat. Accompanying him were a childhood friend and two other young men, who all shared a cabin in a three-week journey to Plymouth in South West England. My father had hoped to see the world, yet within four years he had permanently settled in London. In his third year in the city he met a woman from the northwest of Spain who had also made her home in London. Within a year they were married. A procession of babies, of which I was the last, terminated any ambitions either of them may have had for themselves.

My parents' attitude toward who their children should be, in a country to which they had both migrated, inadvertently rendered me a cultural orphan. I have always felt that I was left unarmed in a society that did not accept me. As an undergraduate, I discovered a small section in the university library on Caribbean literature. It included novels and works of poetry by Indian-Caribbean writers. From these books I learned that I was part of a community and by reading as much as I could, I slowly absorbed the story of indenture in the Caribbean and began a journey that continues to this day.

Two things have shaped the direction of my adult life: my father's silence about his ancestry and the racism that my brothers and I experienced as children of Guyanese-Spanish heritage growing up in West London in the 1970s and 1980s. This was a time when every institution that carried authority attempted to convince immigrant parents that a sense of cultural identity was an obstacle, rather than a lifeline and a necessity. 'You were born here,' my parents would say. 'You're British.' I remember these years as being darkly lit, gloomy. The prevailing attitude of this time in Britain was a bleak one where racism was an everyday experience. My dad was brown and my mother, although white, was not much better. As far as our little island was concerned, they were both 'fucking foreigners.'

For much of my early life, I struggled to understand my father's heritage. As a child, I knew the part of me that was most hated in the place I called home came from him. This never changed the love I had for him. To the contrary, I clung to my connection to his identity as a constant solid thing because I believed I had nothing else. I wasn't Spanish-speaking, I had no Spanish family, and nothing connected me to England beyond the accident of having been born there. In these circumstances, all I could be was my father's daughter. The only thing that people saw when they looked at me was a face that didn't fit; if I wanted a role model in un-belonging, I need not look any further than my father—the progenitor of my incongruity. Yet everything I knew about his background was fragmentary. He was from a country called Guyana. It used to be a British colony. Inexplicably he was both Indian and South American. And this meant that the children who pelted the word 'Paki' at us in the streets were essentially correct. Correct in the sense that this word was used in the UK, as a derogatory term for anyone of South Asian origin.

One night, some neighborhood children threw dog shit against the window of the room that I was sleeping in; this is one of my earliest memories. They had wrapped it in pink toilet paper and some of this paper stuck to the window. There was no joy in the fact that they were forced, either by the police or their parents, to wipe it off the following day. They lived on that street and for the foreseeable future, we would have to see these little fuckers on a weekly basis.

What wears you down more in the end: the big incidents like these? Or, the incessant daily questioning of identity:

'Where are you from?'

'No, where are you really from?'

'But where are you from originally?'

'And before that?'

I understood I wouldn't be permitted to belong to the UK in a myriad of ways. Maybe I was even conscious of it before I could speak. My mum once told me people would shout abuse at her in the streets as she pushed the pram. I wonder how this must have felt for her and for my brothers. They would have been old enough to understand that she was a target because we bore no resemblance to her. Her skin was white, her hair straight and fair and her eyes blue. We, on the other hand, had varying shades of brown skin, brown eyes, and dark brown wavy hair. In my primary and junior school there were no children of South Asian heritage; in my secondary school there were two. If there were South Asian families living in our area, I didn't know any of them. We certainly didn't know any other Guyanese families. There were a lot of Spanish immigrants who made their home in West London in the 1970s and 1980s, but we were so obviously beyond their understanding that there could be no way forward there. Like so many children who have no other way to put themselves in context, I found solace and succor in the local library. I never read a book about anyone like me until I left home to go to university, but in weekly, and sometimes daily, visits I managed to leave a world in which I was largely unaccepted and alone.

I remember the past in snapshots. My dad, perennially exhausted from the oppressive hours he worked as a waiter, was almost always unsmiling. I don't imagine that he intended to be mysterious or unavailable, but he was. I spent a lot of time watching him as a child. I would watch him shave. I would watch him cook. For a man battling the challenge of steering four dual-heritage sons through an institutionally racist country at a time when unemployment rates were high, a daughter who read books must have been a thing of great relief.

My parents' attempts to keep my brothers out of trouble were hampered by their own explosive relationship. Any hopes they had for us were repeatedly dimmed as the two eldest served prison sentences and the two youngest were lost to drugs and alcohol. The next few years were ones where the library became more important to me as I abandoned homework to hide in paper, spines, plastic covers, and stories where I no longer had to inhabit the grey, unrelenting concrete misery of West London. I was fierce on the outside, perennially dressed in black clothes and Doc Martens boots. One October morning, age fifteen, I walked out of school and never went back. Too young to work straight away, I was determined not to return to school. From that autumn, to my birthday in the spring of the next year, I would walk at least twice a week to my local library and then on to Kensington Central Library, which was bigger and had more books. I walked deliberately, absorbed in my Walkman; hopeless, rootless, untethered.

I started full-time work as soon as I was sixteen. The afternoon I told my dad, he sat in a chair with his head in his hands for an hour. I believe he always imagined that what had happened was a hump in the road, a blip. I would go back to school. Many years later he told me about a similar hour he had spent with his father when he was leaving British Guiana to come to England. My father had what I imagined must have been a decent enough job in Georgetown as an apprentice court reporter in the Parliament Building. Why would he want to leave his family and go to a foreign country where he knew no one? After a couple of years, I saw my life ahead of me, doing the same shitty jobs for the same shitty pay; I finally understood that in leaving school so young I had trapped myself. I signed up to a distance learning college and began the long journey to university.

Challenging years followed. I had no study skills, I had been intellectually absent from my short secondary school career and this was never more apparent than when I attempted to write an essay or complete an assignment. I failed as many exams as I passed. In the background I could feel my dad willing me to succeed. Hoping against all present evidence that one of us might be saved. 'Don't be me.' He had silently screamed at us our entire lives. 'Don't drown in this immigrant shit. Be more, be better.' He had told me once that he felt his greatest tragedy was never really knowing what he wanted to do with his life. Any aspirations to explore those desires when he left British Guiana for the UK had been abandoned to take on the harsh reality of supporting a family of five children. Was it easier for him to let his future go because it had never really been fully defined?

And then came the impossible thing, the moment when the years of reading paid off. A succession of failures was obliterated by the reception of an 'A' grade in the Advanced Level English Language and Literature—the exam that got me into university. This was easily the most important moment of my life. More so than any moment that followed it, including completing a doctorate. It was the first tangible proof that a future was possible. I could go to university. That much was clear from this qualification. The blurry outline of an elite institution where I could be blanketed by knowledge was nudged closer and I dared to think I might have a path distinct from that of my brothers; one that did not involve prison, regret, disappointment, and drugs.

As a mature student with a patchy educational history I was summoned for an interview by all six of the universities I applied to. Three of these were outside London and required long train journeys for what amounted to no more than a thirty-minute interview. I remember each of these interviews in great detail; for the first time I was able to talk about my favorite books to people who seemed to love them as much as I did. In train rides to York, Leeds, and Manchester, I felt myself moving forward, away from the past and its shame: the dogshit at the window, the racial abuse, the endless sense that nothing would go right for me. Positive responses trickled back. Royal Holloway, University of London, where I would eventually complete my PhD, gave me an unconditional offer. It was based in Egham, just outside London and this was a problem. It seemed to make sense that I should start a new part of my life in a different city.

In the end I chose Leeds, where I spent the best, but hardest years of my life. In the final term of university, I began to reflect seriously on the question of my cultural identity. I remember a lecturer asking me why my grandfather had 'moved' to British Guiana. I had no idea how to answer this question. I didn't even know whether or not my grandfather had been born in India or British Guiana. In fact, I barely knew or understood what the system of indentured labor was. Having reached my final year of university without dropping out or doing anything that had been expected of me, I earned the right to have questions about the past answered. There were long telephone calls from Leeds to London where my dad would attempt to give satisfactory answers to my questions about his family and how and where he'd grown up. It helped that around this time his two sisters came from Canada to visit him and they made a journey north to see me. The four of us walked around Leeds city center all day, stopping here and there for lunch, for coffee, and talking endlessly about great-grandparents and grandparents. By the end of their visit I had a basic understanding of the paternal side of my father's family. His years of silence about Guyana had ended. My aunts had legitimized my curiosity by answering my questions in front of him. Their stories about my great grandparents filled me with pride and countered the shame racism had taught me to feel as a child. I learned that my father's great grandmother had made the journey to British Guiana alone with a young daughter. The man that her daughter eventually married, my father's paternal grandfather, had achieved near folk-hero status by attacking a bullying plantation overseer and narrowly escaping prison.

Two books bracketed my undergraduate degree, the most important I read as a young person. In my first year as a student I found a copy of Hanif Kureishi's first novel *The Buddha of Suburbia* in a bookshop in the city center. Like many dual-heritage readers before me I was floored by the first line that stood as a challenge to everyone who had questioned my right to articulate my own identity: 'My name is Karim Amir, and I am an Englishman born and bred, almost.'[2] Immediately I was at home in these pages, relieved that I had finally found a book about someone like me—the child of an intercultural marriage trying desperately to stay afloat. Then there was *The Intended* by the Guyanese-born author David Dabydeen. One of the university libraries had an impressive selection of Caribbean literature. Although I didn't need any of the books on these shelves, I had taken to sitting next to them while studying for my penultimate set of exams before graduation. In breaks I could scan the shelves and pull something out without even leaving my chair. I discovered in *The Intended* the story that would decide the course of my eventual academic career.

In *The Intended* I found I was not alone. The novel's depiction of a young Indian-Guyanese boy struggling to make a life for himself as his friends struggled with mental health problems and fell into crime echoed my own experiences growing up with my brothers. By then my frustration with them had ceased and I had begun to understand how much of their behaviour was connected to their sense of unbelonging. I could identify with the main character in his attempts to bury his past and seek sanctuary in study—all the while conscious that the one thing he could never escape was himself. What this book meant to me went beyond the recognition of a representation of my life and the lives of young men I knew growing up in London. It was the first sense that there was something worthy in the narratives of the descendants of indentured laborers. This was a work of fiction about the experiences of indentured immigrants and their descendants. Were there more? The very act of putting this story into the world decimated any lingering ideas I had that my father's silence meant that my history was something to be discarded and abandoned in favor of being 'British.'

In the following weeks I formed the semblance of a plan. I would carry on studying and in the way that they always had, the libraries would help me. I knew the key for me lay in postgraduate study. I took a job in London and worked for a year, all the time searching for universities to apply to. I fell back in love with London as I trawled around antique shops looking for pieces of Guyana's indentured history. I frequently found and bought early twentieth-century postcard images of 'free' and indentured Indian laborers at work in British Guiana. I became aware of the Centre for Caribbean Studies at the University of Warwick and was accepted to pursue a Master of Arts by Research. In 2002, I quit my job and went to Toronto for a few months to spend time with my father's family. There I discovered for the first time an Indian-Caribbean community! I had timed my journey to coincide with the celebration of Indian Arrival Day and was amazed by the number of Canadians of Indian-Guyanese descent who were interested in their history. Was my dad just an anomaly? I read books, of course, lots of them, most memorably *A House for Mr. Biswas* by V. S. Naipaul, which made me ache with both pride and the pain of recognition. For the first time I ate pepperpot, souse, black pudding, and curry with roti. My strongest thought during this trip to Toronto concerned how and when I might travel to Guyana. With no family that I knew of living there, this seemed like an impossible task. Yet I was determined to go. I had stumbled through much of my life and now something had changed—I had a sense of history and I was on a mission to contribute something positive, to honor the exceptional men and women who were part of my family story.

The year at Warwick passed in a blur. I was exhausted all the time; a job on campus as a cleaner provided me an opportunity to pay my major expenses and in this vital year, I learned how to be a researcher. Bouncing around London's archives, I felt as though I were putting the pieces of a jigsaw together, poring over resources to recover a particular piece of indentured history. I completed my MA on the minority South Indian community of Guyana, exploring their presence in the indenture system and studying their religious traditions and literature. During the course of this research, I learned that my father's maternal grandfather was the son of an indentured laborer from South India. The very fact that I now had access to a family who wanted to talk to me about their childhood visits to the Kali Mai Puja (a significant South Indian festival in Guyana) was a world away from the cultural silence that I had been stifled by as a child. A kindly Guyanese writer of South Indian heritage living in England, Peter Kempadoo, agreed to allow me to interview him in his Coventry home. 'Where are you from?' he had asked me on the phone before we met. When I replied that I was the product of a Guyanese-Spanish alliance he laughed: 'Ah, then you're what we call a "mix-up girl!"' While this was undoubtedly the case, what I was no longer was a mixed-up girl. That period of my life was over.

Then in 2006 came Guyana. I registered at Royal Holloway to complete my PhD. It was inconceivable that I could continue my work without visiting Guyana's archives. My husband was the son of a man who had spent his life travelling. Consequently, he was instrumental in convincing me it could be done. Straight away my father told me he was coming with us and by the end of the month we had accrued five more returning family members. The first week I felt lost and longed to leave. I marveled at my husband, a Scotch-Ghanaian born in Lesotho and brought-up in Malawi, as he strolled around Georgetown in the manner of a man who had never lived anywhere else. Yet I quickly came around. For a girl who had barely left London, seeing the interior of Guyana for the first time from a tiny airplane was indescribable. Although I never managed to find the documents I sought in the archives, I was happy to make unexpected connections with the people I met in the city, my father's old school friend, distant cousins, librarians, and archivists.

The morning we arrived we went to see a first cousin of my father's, Aunty Meena. I cannot forget her changing expression as an uncle patiently reminded her of a journey she had made with her mother in 1961 to wave off a boat that was carrying a young man, her relative, to England. Slowly I saw it dawn on her as she repeated, each time more confidently: 'Me remember you, me remember you.' I cherished our visits with this aunt who appeared to love me for no other reason than that I was somehow her kin.

Our time in Guyana was over so quickly. And yet, forty-five years had passed since my father left. I think that he must have believed he would die without seeing the country again. A taxi took us to the airport. I didn't realize that from the back of the car my husband had taken a video of us leaving. In one scene, my head is poking out of the window in the back seat as I strain to get a last look. My father, sitting in the front seat, is smiling. I imagine that this was the smile of a man of little means, who after revisiting the land of his birth realized that he did after all have something of value to give to one of his children.

Figure 13.2

My father's return to Guyana in 2006 after forty-five years. Photo by David V. Y. Wallis. Maria del Pilar Kaladeen Family Collection.

Bibliography

Dabydeen, David, *The Intended* (London: Martin Secker and Warburg, 1991).

Kureishi, Hanif, *The Buddha of Suburbia* (London: Faber and Faber, 1990).

Naipul, V. S., *A House for Mrs. Biswas* (London: André Deutsch, 1961).

Notes

1. The phrase 'Windrush Generation' refers to a period of large-scale migration from the Caribbean to the United Kingdom. Roughly, this movement of people took place from 1948 through 1971. For more information, see 'Postface: A Brief History of Migration from Guyana.'

2. Hanif Kureishi, *The Buddha of Suburbia* (London: Faber and Faber, 1990), p. 3.

14.

Keeping Wake

—

Maya Mackrandilal

Figure 14.1

My family farm in Mahaicony, Demerara, Guyana. Maya Mackrandilal, *Up Mahaicony*, 2011, digital photography.

In the summer of 2011, I was awarded a grant to travel to Guyana, my mother's country of birth. It was the first time I had visited since 1997 (I was twelve), and the first time I had made the trip on my own. As an American-born artist, I had been researching stories of Guyanese migration

 https://doi.org/10.11647/OBP.0218.18

for quite some time, collecting interviews with older extended family members as well as my grandmother (Nanie in Hindi) and mother. The eldest of twelve children, my mother first left Guyana in 1976 to attend the University of Guelph in Ontario, Canada for her Master's degree. She then migrated to the United States in 1978 to work for the World Bank. The rest of her siblings immigrated to the US over the years, except for one uncle, who stayed behind to tend to the family rice farm.

During my trip, I visited our family's farm in Mahaicony, a small rural community on the banks of the Mahaicony River along Guyana's coast in Demerara county. Many of its inhabitants are descendants of South Asian indentured laborers who became rice farmers after their term of indenture, which is how my grandfather's family became established in the region. While I was on our farm with my uncle, we got news that my grandmother, now living with one of my aunts in New York, had a brain aneurysm, eventually passing away. Suddenly my solitary trip became a family affair, with aunts, uncles, and cousins returning from their homes in the United States to lay my grandmother to rest next to my grandfather on the farm.

My grandmother was the daughter of a man of Indian descent who converted from Hinduism to Islam to marry his second wife. My grandmother's mother (the third wife) was a Christian woman of Chinese, African, and European heritage. My grandmother wanted to be a schoolteacher, but became a farmer's wife instead, fulfilling a promise she made to her father before he died to marry my grandfather. Once married, she focused on family and community, keeping a collection of books that local children were welcome to read and borrow.

What follows is a poetic and artistic meditation on our family's intersecting stories. Like ripples of water, they collide with my body in amplifications and erasures. The accompanying images are mixed media works. While in the farmhouse in Mahaicony, I came across family albums with images of my grandmother, aunts, cousins, and other members of the community. Because of the humidity, the photographs had fused with the album pages, making them difficult or impossible to remove without damage. I created digital images of these photographs, which were then printed with an inkjet printer and manipulated with water and paint to mimic how the humid air of the farmhouse will further degrade the original photographs over time. These images, and the sometimes abstracted nature of the text itself, are expressions of the histories that have been lost to time and memory, the realities we gloss over, the names we forget, and the feelings that remain as our heritage is passed from one body to the next.

*

Motion Sickness

There is a particular ritual: face forward, keep eyes on the horizon, breathe deeply—but it can fail. I am on the train, the bus, a car, a plane, suddenly overcome, lightheaded, nauseous.

I wonder if my body's reaction to motion is the legacy of my foremothers. The trace of their fear (encoded in flesh) as they moved across the globe like cargo.

What would happen if our bodies retraced their paths? Could we become divining rods for truth?

They made vagrancy a crime to keep slaves on the estates. To keep them tied to the land; the land was servitude. Even when they were 'freed' they were still tied to the land and through the land to their masters. Is this why we are nomads? Why we never had a home?

Nanie Says:

'Land is like gold.'

My Body Is a Reluctant Nomad

My body rebelled in ways nobody could quantify. All the doctors could agree on was that it was 'safer' for me not to go. Nanie kept her opinion to herself and embroidered on the deck beside me silently as I pondered the relationality of the body, how my health was suddenly dependent on something as abstract as national boundaries. Aunts called, concerned for my safety in a land they once called home. Nanie bought canned sardines, coffee, and toothpaste for me to bring to Uncle on the farm. I bought the latest issue of *The New Yorker* to read on the plane.

A year later I watched my mother take her oath of citizenship. A video of President Barack Obama welcomed her. A friend remarked: 'this place is like a DMV for people.' How could I believe that for the first twenty-seven years of my life my mother was fundamentally different from me, a difference that accorded me more rights, more freedoms, more agency? How could I believe that by standing in that room under fluorescent lights and raising her hand she was casting off one identity for another? Our bodies cannot lie—this I choose to believe.

A Savage Womb

Each wave, the sickness spreads. Fear eats at her body with each mile she is not herself. There is a new kinship—awake, the scent of home (damp earth, smoky blankets, splintered stone) fades from her skin, replaced by blood, sweat, and bile.

Licked clean.

Only after would come the sugar cane fields watered with sweat and the sweet intoxication as, distilled, it burned warm in her chest.

All she wants to do is be a cannibal; spit up a new history; never die. She wants to be told.

Momme Says:

Yeah, I don't know why we never asked my grandmother these things. I once read this book called *L'Enfant Noir* about this guy, and he said, 'when we were young all the questions we should have asked we never asked' and I guess part of our problem was that we never were really that interested in our past, because we always felt that there were things that we really didn't want to know, and it was only the future that mattered, so we never really asked about these things . . .

A Promise is a Promise

I think there is a kind of truce between Nanie and me. I'm not sure when it happened. The clicking of her knitting needles and her disapproval of me permeate my childhood memories. Always too loud, too opinionated, too stubborn. As if these things were not my inheritance. As if they were not the things that kept our foremothers alive.

I asked Nanie to tell me her life story once. When she got to the subject of my grandfather, she said that she had other offers of marriage. My grandfather had said 'a promise is a promise' and she had agreed.

A promise. A deep black pool that contains the future and the past. All the things unsaid, to be lost in the faulty memories of those who survive.

Figure 14.2
Maya Mackrandilal, 'Keeping Wake I'

2014, mixed media with found images on artboard.

A Brief History of the Body

Nanie: My *Aaji*, Ramsuki. She say she was just a little girl, gone to get some water from a well. Someone snatch she, marauders or the like. Sell she to the British.

(On the boat, the women knew she needed to be protected. There was a man. In some stories he is a paying passenger, a free man, a wandering *sadhu*. He agrees to marry her. The captain says some words, then she goes back to stay with the women for the rest of the trip.)

Nanie: When they land, she sent to plantation, name Success. They give she a *loji*, a place to live, like. He stay with she, but he don't work, don't take care of the children. She working the cane fields all day, he sleepin.

Nanie: Eventually he abandons Ramsuki, goes to Suriname to be a holy man.

Momme: She kicked him out for being lazy.

History with a capital H

I flip carefully through the book, scanning the endless rows and columns of names. Each entry is an anchor slowly fading from the page. I already know I won't find what I'm looking for, the stern lady at the desk tells me that the particular volume of birth records for the place and time I'm looking for is 'missing.' When I ask what that means she just rolls her eyes. I lie and say I need this year to look for a separate entry. I come to a series of pages where the names cascade away into a creamy white void. The book was exposed to water at some point, and over a hundred entries must be missing. Bloodlines lost forever to a spilled cup or a heavy rain. This is the legacy of our ancestors' trauma, all the little things we will never know.

Landing

From above, the water looks like a giant knife cut a dark winding gash through the land. On the ground, our boat rumbles to a start—everything seems soft, overripe. The creek water is almost black, so rich with particles that your hand disappears completely once the water reaches your elbow. It's hard to speak above the air rushing past and the roar of the motor. Occasionally Uncle points and yells something, but mostly I just watch the banks glide by. It seems like everything is melting into everything else, the boundary between water and land unclear.

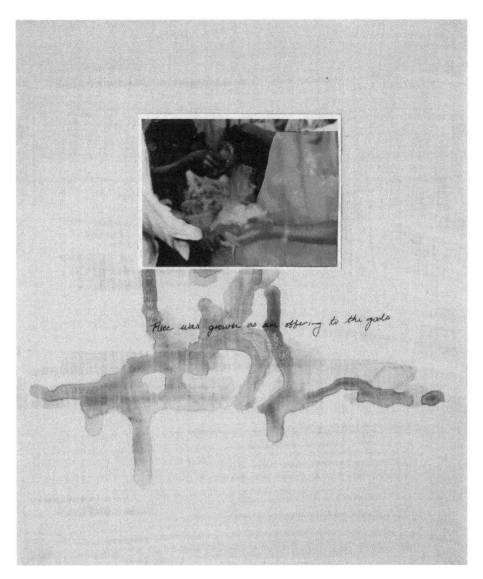

Figure 14.3
Maya Mackrandilal, 'Keeping Wake II'
2014, mixed media with found images on artboard.

When I was younger, I was afraid to swim in the water, stories of close calls with alligators and piranhas turning every ripple into a threat. Auntie is not helping, telling the story of the time she hitched a ride home from school with a neighbor who was drunk, and how she, her younger sister, and a friend, had all nearly drowned when the boat crashed. The friend had panicked and pulled her sister under. Auntie said she just reached blindly down into the black and pulled her sister up by the bow in her hair.

We're on the back verandah of the house, the rice fields stretching out endlessly before us, the canal my grandfather dug off the creek to our right. My mother has her own story of almost drowning, my great-grandmother pulling her unconscious from the water. I think of this silent, black void flowing behind us, and the countless stories of being pulled from it by hands that knew no fear.

As a last resort, a slave could take his life, knowing that this was his final revenge; to deny the master the thing he prized most, his property.[1]

Kal Pani

I
They called the sea *Kal Pani*—black water. They said if you crossed it, you lost caste— you became forever severed from your life, from the land. I often wonder what they must have thought, emerging from the tomb-like ships, to a land with such unctuous rivers—rivers that on certain still evenings take on the quality of black glass—a river of ink—*kal pani*.

II
Blood is mostly water, a means of transporting oxygen and nutrients around the body. It's strange that for some people it is transferable, shareable, and for others it is more particular. A mechanism and a fingerprint—*lal pani*.

III
Uncle tells me the river changes course with the tides. The land breathes like a lung.

IV
I think of Nanie's brain, the flood of *lal pani* from a ruptured aneurysm. I think of the mysteries locked in our blood, the stories of our bodies, permeating her brain. Maybe for a moment before she lost consciousness she got some insight, some answer that can only be found in water.

V

They flood the rice fields in the planting season. I wonder how we came up with the concept of parallel lines, of corners. Why do we so naturally lean towards this type of efficiency? Nature is efficient in a completely different kind of way. A way that seems infinite and non-linear. Squares lead to fields, lead to blocks, lead to buildings, lead to temples lead to hierarchy and history and war. Curved lines don't really lead anywhere, except that they are blood cells and bubbles and planets.

VI

Thalassa, the sea, *haema*, blood. *Thalassemia*, sea blood.

VII

Walcott said the sea is history. My blood is sea blood. My blood is fractured, thrown outside of time. How to live from one moment to the next is a question I can't answer, just as I don't know if you can step in the same river twice.

VIII

Nanie asked that we build her tomb high above the ground so the flooding river would not touch her body. In India they cremate remains and submerge the ashes in the Ganges. Embrace the void or embrace the land, in-between is life.

An Atlas in the Sand

We ride out in the boat, picking up some friends along the way. We pass beneath rusting bridges that you can almost reach up and touch. Sometimes, people on the banks wave to us. The open farmland gives way to trees that lean over us from the banks. All of a sudden, the motor slows and the banks throw themselves wide to embrace the Atlantic.

(Sea of Atlas, who stands between the primordial embrace of earth and sky.)

At low tide the beach is wide, the land creeping from the ocean at the lowest possible angle. The men head off into the trees to pull crabs with their bare hands from the tidal pools that form around the roots.

I head out across the alien landscape, passing twisted roots knotted into a ball and bleached by the sun. As the tide recedes, it leaves ripples across the sand. I stand at the water line and watch the water lap slowly towards my toes. I look over my shoulder and see Uncle and his friends up by the trees, drinking rum and eating food. They remind me of an old picture I found in the farmhouse, the figures dark and haloed by the sun.

I look back out across the water. The air is still and smells fresh, not salty. I think of deep ocean currents swirling across the globe. I wonder how long it would take a drop of water to travel from India to Guyana. Is it faster, or slower than a ship with sails? I chant the Gayatri Mantra to the water, not sure where my words will come to rest.

The long-boned, stalwart Bhojpuri, with his staff in hand, is a familiar object striding over fields far from home.

Lal Pani

Uncle is something of a sentinel, trapped in a liminal space between the past and the future. As the eldest son, he had to leave school young to help with the farm. Nanie would say that when he drove the tractor in the field, he was so small it looked like the tractor was driving itself. Nanie had ten daughters but only two sons, and Uncle, bound to the farm, and through the farm bound to Guyana, tied up in an endless cycle of planting and reaping, was a stone caught in her throat.

Rice was grown as an offering to the gods.

It is the day after our boat trip. In the morning I work with clay collected from the trenches that line the rice fields, shaping it in my hands. I lay it out in the sun to dry, burnishing the surface with the back of a spoon. The neighbor says it reminds her of when they were children, that they would make small things with mud. After dinner I spend the evening in the sitting room, reading and writing in my journal. Uncle emerges from the bedroom, his eyes red. He tells me Nanie is in the hospital. They say it's a brain aneurysm. There's no internet out here, his cell phone is our only connection. I feel lost in the warm, still night. Part of me knows she is already gone, though her body continues to live for another day in the hospital as her children gather to say goodbye.

Keeping Wake

I never imagined death was such a complicated thing. Nanie's body must be prepared, dressed. My mother is the eldest child. She and Auntie wrap their mother in a white sari. Meanwhile, on the farm, I am the only family Uncle has. Every night the neighbors come to 'keep wake.' I sit upstairs listening to the rhythmic crack as dominoes are slammed against tables. The women play cards with children and we serve bread and coffee late into the night. I don't know the games, don't know the people, I feel more alien now than ever before. The mosquitos flock to me in the cool night air, so I stay inside, alone.

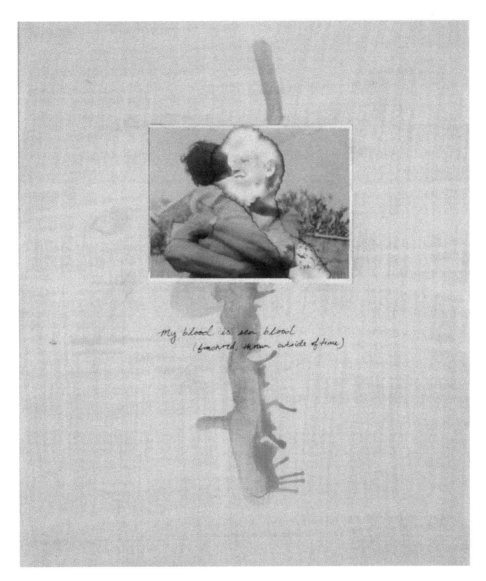

Figure 14.4

Maya Mackrandilal, 'Keeping Wake III'

2014, mixed media with found images on artboard.

During the day neighbors come to work, clearing brush, cleaning out the sheds, building out a shelter off the side of the house my grandfather built by hand. There are men out by his grave, building my grandmother's tomb from cinder blocks and cement.

I gather scraps of wood. I dig a pit and place my clay objects, wrapped in newspaper, along the bottom. I build a small fire on top. In the evening I pull the fired pieces from the ash.

. . . the Indians exchanged a society and a living community (though unequal and degrading to many, tiresome and tedious to most) for a lifeless system, in which human values always mattered less than the drive for production, for exploitation.

A few days later some of Uncle's friends take me back to the city. My family comes in waves, and soon we are all there. We have a funeral in the city, and then drive out to the farm. The dirt road is a recent addition. Before coffins had to be carried the last stretch by boat.

Embracing the Void

There is nothing left to inherit
Locked away in your body
All that is left
Is your wake
Cutting through these dark waters
Lapping
against the shorelines of memory

Before the coffin is closed, I slip one of my clay objects, a palm-sized Ganesh, next to Nanie's body.

Tumhi ho mata
Pita tumhi ho
Tumhi ho bandhu
Sakha tumhi ho

The old women begin to sing, their voices outside of time.
Our understanding of the words is imprecise
But my mother's voice cracks
And I hold her, sobbing, in my arms.

Figure 14.5

Maya Mackrandilal, 'Keeping Wake IV'

2014, mixed media with found images on artboard.

Later, the sun is setting. We don't have swimsuits, so we bathe in our clothes.
Together we wade out on the plank in front of the house
And in the fading light we almost feel like a family again (this feeling will soon fade).
My cousin and I swim out into the black water, our bodies floating in the void
Working against the pull of the current out to sea.

Notes

1. Italics in English here and below are either direct quotes or paraphrased lines from Hugh Tinker, *A New System of Slavery: The Export of Indian Labour Overseas 1830–1920* (London and New York: Oxford University Press, 1974).

Postface:
A Brief History of Migration from Guyana

—

Grace Aneiza Ali

Guyana *is* historically a country of migrations. And continues to be in a contemporary state of flux. As a multi-cultural nation of Amerindians, British, Portuguese, Africans, Indians, and Chinese, Guyana is the only English-speaking country in South America. The country's religious landscape equally reflects its dynamic population: Christian, Muslim, Hindu, and Catholic, among others. In the present day, the Guyanese diaspora can be found in the global metropolises of London, New York City, and Toronto.

Guyana's location in the northeastern region of the continent, in the heart of the Amazon rainforest—coupled with a history of British colonization that it shares with nearby Caribbean islands—allows for the nation's hybrid cultural identity between Caribbean and South American. From the sixteenth to the nineteenth century, Guyana's lands were subjected to European explorers and colonists, its territory changing hands among the Spanish, Portuguese, Dutch, and, finally, the British empire. From the early 1600s to the 1800s, the British utilized the enslavement of Africans in their vigorous pursuit of wealth via sugar production. When slavery was abolished in 1834, the British instituted the system of indentured servitude that lasted until 1917, bringing Indian and Chinese laborers into the colony—a measure that would later define Guyana's modern multi-cultural landscape and also set the tone for decades of ethnic conflict between Africans and Indians. Often violent and politically explosive, the ethnic tensions fueled and exploited by the British themselves would scar Guyana throughout the twentieth and twenty-first centuries.

Guyana now has a population of 787,000 and over one million living in its diaspora—an exodus that began as early as the 1940s. In 1948, the British Nationality Act gave British citizenship to all people living in its commonwealth countries and full rights of entry and settlement in Britain. Throughout the 1950s and 1960s, many ambitious dreamers in British Guiana took advantage of the British Nationality Act and began making their way to England. As the first significant group of Caribbean

    https://doi.org/10.11647/OBP.0218.19

immigrants to arrive in Britain, they became known as the 'Windrush Generation,' after the SS Empire Windrush, the inaugural ship that brought the first Caribbean immigrants to Tilbury Dock in Essex, England in 1948.

They left because it was necessary that they imagine a world beyond British Guiana. At that time, there was no university in the colony. For example, the University of Guyana (UG), the first of its kind in the country, was established only in 1963 and initially offered limited evening classes under British governance. A desire for professional and economic advancement inevitably meant migration. The early 1950s would become a period rife with intense political unrest as the movement towards gaining independence became more forceful. Throughout the 1940s and 1950s, Guyanese immigrants primarily chose Britain as their destination—a choice that made sense to many as the colony was still under British rule. However, a backlash against the increasing number of the colonies' Caribbean-born workers and their families moving into Britain's neighborhoods led to the 1962 Commonwealth Immigration Act, which would overturn the Nationality Act of 1948, citing it as an unregulated approach to immigration.

In the mid-1950s, another movement of migration to North America unfolded as Guyanese became part of a larger trend of Caribbean people, particularly those from the British colonies, shifting to the United States and Canada and specifically to urban cities like New York and Toronto, respectively. In April of 1953, the colony had undergone its first democratic election and yet it would take another thirteen volatile years, marked by highly oppressive policies by the elected government, before gaining independence in 1966.

Many did not wait and orchestrated their own independence. With new restrictions placed on migrating to the United Kingdom, Guyanese then turned to the US. The US Immigration and Nationality Act of 1965 had removed prior conditions that restricted entry into the US based on race and ethnicity quotas and skilled labor, making it easier for Guyanese citizens to migrate to the US. In fact, the 1965 Act ushered in a great wave of immigration to the US from all over the world. Seeing America as their new 'El Dorado'—the new land of opportunity—from the 1950s to present day, the US has steadfastly remained the largest diasporic node for Guyanese. The majority of Guyanese immigrants leaving Guyana still choose to make the US their home, particularly New York City, where Guyanese immigrants now make up the city's fifth largest immigrant population. In the 1970s and 1980s, another movement of emigration unfolded as Guyanese began shifting to Canada. By 2001, Toronto emerged as a prominent node in the Caribbean diaspora as one of the largest and oldest Guyanese populations outside of Guyana.

List of Illustrations

Introduction

Chapter 1

Chapter 2

Chapter 3

Chapter 4

Chapter 5

Chapter 6

Chapter 7

Chapter 8

Chapter 9

Chapter 10

Chapter 11

Chapter 12

Chapter 13

Chapter 14

Acknowledgments

I am deeply grateful to many who, over the course of the journey to usher this book into the world, showed unending support and generosity. First, I am indebted to the fifteen women gathered in this collection for lending their brilliant art and words to this project. And, I am always centered and buoyed by the abiding love of my beloveds: Ingrid Ali, Candace Ali-Lindsay, Vanya Lindsay, Stephen Ali, Grandma Alice Luckey, and Cosmo Whyte.

In the early days of this project, I began writing Chapter 4, 'The Geography of Separation,' under the tutelage of a memoir workshop taught by the great Hettie Jones—an experience I hold dear to my heart. I also thank literary agent Faith Childs for being a fervent champion of bringing this project to light.

At New York University, I thank Kathy Engel for her gracious mentorship and the faculty and staff of the Department of Art & Public Policy for the thriving scholarly community they engender. I thank Dr. Deborah Willis for her meaningful gestures to be inclusive of Guyana as she charts innovative scholarship on women, art, photography, and migration, and for her invitation to contribute to *Women and Migration: Responses in Art and History* (2019). I am grateful for the support of the Office of the Provost, particularly the Provost's Postdoctoral Fellowship Program and the support of Charlton McIlwain, Cybele Raver, and Farooq Niazi. This book is freely available in an open access edition thanks to the support of the Office of Global Inclusion and the Dean's Office at the Tisch School of the Arts, Dean Allyson Green, Fred Carl, and Karen Shimakawa.

I thank the following friends, colleagues and institutions for their guidance and unwavering work to elevate Guyanese writing, art and culture in this project and beyond: Kate Angus, Gaiutra Bahadur, Patrick Bova, Alessandra Benedicty, Maria Magdalena Campos-Pons, David Dabydeen, Victor Davson, Celeste Hamilton Dennis, Erin Haney, Terrence Jennings, Roshini Kempadoo, Oneka LaBennett, Brenda Locke, Allen McFarlane, E. Ethelbert Miller, Khalil Gibran Muhammad, Pamela Newkirk, Zita Nunes, Samuel Roberts, Karen Wharton, and the Andy Warhol Foundation for the Visual Arts, Aljira, a Center for Contemporary Art, and Caribbean Cultural Center African Diaspora Institute.

Finally, Alessandra Tosi and her talented team at Open Book Publishers showed this project the utmost care, thoughtfulness, and generosity. I am thankful to them beyond measure.

The Publishing Team

Alessandra Tosi was the managing editor for this book.

Adele Kreager performed the copy-editing, proofreading and the indexing.

Linda Florio and Anna Gatti designed the cover using InDesign. The image featured on the cover is Grace Aneiza Ali, *The SeaWall*, Georgetown, Guyana (2014). Digital photo by Candace Ali-Lindsay. Courtesy of the artist, CC BY-NC-ND. The cover was produced in InDesign using Fontin (titles) and Calibri (text body) fonts.

Luca Baffa typeset the book in InDesign. The text is set in Libre Baskerville. Luca created all of the editions—paperback, hardback, EPUB, MOBI, PDF, HTML, and XML. The conversion was performed with open source software freely available on our GitHub page (https://github.com/OpenBookPublishers).

This book need not end here . . .

Share

All our books—including the one you have just read—are free to access online so that students, researchers and members of the public who can't afford a printed edition will have access to the same ideas. This title will be accessed online by hundreds of readers each month across the globe: why not share the link so that someone you know is one of them?

This book and additional content is available at: https://doi.org/10.11647/OBP.0218

Customise

Personalise your copy of this book or design new books using OBP and third-party material. Take chapters or whole books from our published list and make a special edition, a new anthology or an illuminating coursepack. Each customised edition will be produced as a paperback and a downloadable PDF.

Find out more at: https://www.openbookpublishers.com/section/59/1

You may also be interested in:

Women and Migration

Responses in Art and History

Deborah Willis, Ellyn Toscano and Kalia Brooks Nelson (eds)

https://doi.org/10.11647/OBP.0153

Essays on Paula Rego

Smile When You Think about Hell

Maria Manuel Lisboa

https://doi.org/10.11647/OBP.0178

Mobilities, Boundaries, and Travelling Ideas

Rethinking Translocality Beyond Central Asia and the Caucasus

Manja Stephan-Emmrich and Philipp Schröder (eds)

https://doi.org/10.11647/OBP.0114

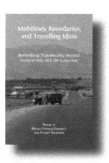

Frontier Encounters

Knowledge and Practice at the Russian, Chinese and Mongolian Border

Franck Billé, Grégory Delaplace and Caroline Humphrey (eds)

https://doi.org/10.11647/OBP.0026

CPSIA information can be obtained
at www.ICGtesting.com
Printed in the USA
BVHW022107281020
591899BV00002B/31